ALAN MOOREHEAD

No Room in the Ark

WITH SIXTEEN PLATES

PENGUIN BOOKS

IN ASSOCIATION WITH

HAMISH HAMILTON

Penguin Books Ltd, Harmondsworth, Middlesex, England
Penguin Books Australia Ltd, Ringwood, Victoria, Australia

—

First published in Great Britain by Hamish Hamilton 1959
Published in Penguin Books 1962
Reprinted 1963, 1964, 1968

—

Copyright © Alan Moorehead, 1957, 1958, 1959

—

Made and printed in Great Britain
by Hazell Watson & Viney Ltd,
Aylesbury, Bucks
Set in Linotype Pilgrim

TO

Major-General
Sir Francis De Guingand

Dear Freddie,

I had made one or two flying visits to Africa below the Sahara before I came to stay with you in Johannesburg in 1956, but it was only then that I began to explore in earnest. Now Africa is in the blood and I begin to understand what Joseph Thomson meant when he wrote just before he died, 'I am doomed to be a wanderer. I am not an empire-builder, I am not a missionary. I am not truly a scientist. I merely want to return to Africa to continue my wanderings.'

Not much perhaps is left of Thomson's Africa now, but I feel that on four journeys during the last few years I have had a glimpse of that lost world you knew so well when you were a young officer in the King's African Rifles.

We will forget and forgive the deplorable days when you were out with a rifle shooting elephants and hoping to pay for your leave with the ivory; I believe you to have become a reformed character since then. And so I hope that you will approve of what you find here, for I would like to inscribe this book to you and to acknowledge myself, as ever,

Yours affectionately,

Alan Moorehead

CONTENTS

NOTE   9

1 THE WELL-GROOMED BABOON   11
2 THE HYRAX IN ARCADIA   37
3 A PLEISTOCENE DAY   73
4 THE OTHER SIDE OF THE HILL   89
5 THE POISONED ARROW   109
6 A MOST FORGIVING APE   124
7 THE KARAMOJONG   135
8 SINCE MAYERLING   161
9 THE NILE   182

MAPS
     AFRICA   220–1
     EAST AFRICA   222–3

NOTE

IT would be quite impossible to acknowledge here by name all those who helped me on my journeys through Southern and Eastern Africa, for it is one of the most hospitable regions on earth and the traveller there, once he leaves the cities, is very much dependent upon the kindness of the residents.

I must, however, offer my particular thanks to Captain Potter, of the Hluhluwe reserve in South Africa, to Mervyn Cowie, Noel Simon, David Sheldrick, Hugh Massey, Donald Ker, and Sidney Downey in Kenya, to Peter Molloy in Tanganyika, to Ralph Dreschfield, Rennie Bere, Frank Poppleton, Bombo Trimmer, Bruce Kinloch, Major Robson, and John Blower in Uganda.

All these men in one way or another are concerned with the protection of what is left of the wild life in Africa. For the moment this is a losing battle, and although I know that none of them has yet lost heart it is only fair that they and their colleagues should be reminded that there are very many of us scattered about the world who know something of the struggle they are making and who look upon it with admiration and respect. I never met a game warden in Africa, or anyone connected with the national parks, who was in the job for any other reason than that he loved the work and believed in it; and this perhaps more than anything else leads one to hope that they will not be defeated in the end.

The illustrations in this book have come from a number of different sources. Most of the photographs have been supplied by my old friend George Rodger and others like him, who have travelled widely in Africa with a sensitive and sympathetic eye. Plates 6 and 7 were supplied by Mrs H. Stevenson Hamilton.

Miss Freya Stark and Captain Charles R. S. Pitman have kindly read the proofs.

NOTE

There remains one other acknowledgement to be made, and that is to the editor of the *New Yorker*, in whose columns much of what is written in the following pages first appeared, though in a somewhat different form. He has readily consented to the re-publication of this material, and I would like to thank him.

The book has also been serialized in the *Sunday Times*.

A.M.

CHAPTER ONE

THE WELL-GROOMED BABOON

YEARS ago the British used to run a flying-boat service down through Africa, and although it was a slow and sometimes rather bumpy journey I can remember no flight that was quite so pleasant. You took off from Cairo in the early morning with a fine rush of water spurting past the portholes, and then by easy stages followed the Nile upstream to its source in Lake Victoria on the Equator. Thence the route followed a series of lakes along the Great Rift Valley until eventually you reached Durban in South Africa. There was no flying after dark, and the machine put down at some fascinating places on the way: Wadi Halfa in the midst of the Egyptian desert, Khartoum at the junction of the Blue and the White Niles in the Sudan, Kisumu on Lake Victoria (the lake itself so big that you lost sight of the shore as you flew across it), and Livingstone, just a mile or two above the Victoria Falls.

Most of these stops were out-of-the-way places which had very little connexion with the outside world, and so you were plunged at once into the authentic African scene. There were no familiar airport buildings, no advertisements, no other traffic of any kind; just this rush of muddy water as you lighted down on a river or a forest lake, and the boy who came out in a boat to take you to the shore was the genuine article, a coal black African, sometimes naked to the waist. He looked as though he would have been really more at home in a thatched hut than in this strange world of flying monsters in the sky.

On the Zambezi River I recall they had to run a launch up and down the water a few minutes before the plane came in to clear the hippopotami away. I remember too, with particular vividness, a little place called Malakal on the White Nile in the Sudan, where the women of the

Dinka tribe were six foot tall and as hipless as young boys. Their hair was thickly matted with grease and piled up in a marvellous coiffure high above their heads. They walked gravely along the river bank and turned their heads away from the great flying-boat on the water in the way that primitive people often do when they are confronted with something which they regard as quite miraculous and beyond all comprehension.

These scenes gave the passenger a brief but very potent whiff of Africa. He felt he was seeing the country as Livingstone and the other early explorers had seen it, and although I made this journey only once and as long ago as 1941 it filled me with an intense desire to come back one day. Most of all I wanted to see the animals, and after that some of the less frequented places from the Congo southwards – black Africa below the bulge. It was, I suppose, nothing more than the usual tourist thirst for the Africa of the tribal drums and the jungle in the raw, but it was none the less genuine for that. The war, however, soon put a stop to any notions of this kind, and for one reason or another I kept putting off the trip until one day a year or two ago in London I happened to meet a friend who lived in South Africa. He asked me to come and stay with him in Johannesburg; everything, he said, could be arranged from there. Within ten days my wife and I set off.

Compared to the old flying-boat days the present journey by air to South Africa is rather a humdrum affair, and Johannesburg itself has a sobering effect on anyone who arrives, as we did, with somewhat highly-charged ideas about the primitiveness of Africa. We had not been in the city twenty-four hours before we found ourselves being disillusioned on two quite definite points. There were, we were told, very few large wild animals in South Africa any more – wild, that is, in the sense of roaming about the countryside at will. As recently as eighty or ninety years ago they teemed in millions; on the very place where the new city of Johannesburg now stands (it is barely seventy years old), the early farmers record seeing hordes of spring-bok half a mile wide that took four hours to pass. They were shot down by the wagon-load, and the carcasses sold off for sixpence apiece. The springbok is a lovely antelope that proceeds in times of danger with a series of immense bounds into the air, and it is the national symbol of South Africa. Today, however, you would be lucky to see even a single specimen anywhere around Johannesburg; along with the other wild animals the species has only been pre-served in the game sanctuaries and the National Parks. Other creatures like the quagga, the Cape lion, and the blue buck are now altogether extinct.

Our other disillusionment was concerned with the primi-tive African communities we were so anxious to see : the noble naked huntsman with his bow and arrow, his war dances, and his witch doctory. I consulted an English woman who had been living in Africa for many years about this. 'I doubt,' she said, 'if you will find many Africans going *naked* any more. Up north in Uganda you may come across a few tribes where the women wear only a clump of leaves tied around their waists. But there are not very many of them. All Africans prefer to wear European clothes if they can get them, and to hunt with rifles and shotguns instead of spears. As for the dancing, the best place to see it is at the gold mines here in Johannesburg. The miners put on a show on Sunday mornings – but not naked of course. They wear their miners' helmets and the shirts and trousers in which they work.'

'But the bushmen,' I said. 'The primitive bushmen in the Kalahari desert?'

'Well yes,' she replied, 'they *are* rather primitive, but unless you are an anthropologist I don't think you would find them very interesting. They don't actually do any-thing, you see. Most of the time they sit around in a circle grubbing for wild melons in the ground. Just occasionally a man will get to his feet and shuffle around in a kind of slow dance for a bit, but that is the only thing that ever happens. They don't even breed any more.'

All this was very disappointing, and I confess that as my wife and I wandered about Johannesburg and the neighbouring countryside for the first week or so we saw nothing that would have seemed really remarkable in Manchester or Birmingham. This was a world of tenements and office blocks, of golf-courses and suburban gardens, of shanty towns and gas stations; and it is only occasionally that something happens to remind you that this is still Africa, and that it hasn't yet been altogether overtaken by the outside world. One hot evening my host and I went for a walk, and we might have been in any pleasant garden suburb anywhere except that, as we turned a corner, we found ourselves in the midst of a stampede of young Negro boys. They ran past us with frantic staring expressions on their faces, and two African policemen came after them, shouting as they ran. We soon saw what had been happening: the young Negroes had been breaking the law by playing cards in the street. There, scattered on the grass, were the cards, a straw hat and a jacket abandoned by their owners in their haste to get away, a wallet that had fallen to the ground. When the police saw that there was no hope of catching the young men they stopped and picked up these fallen objects. Then they went back to their prison van and began calling out softly: 'Here's your wallet. If you want it come and get it. Here's your jacket.'

The young men turned round and stood uncertainly in the roadway. Obviously it was quite unbearable to them to see their precious things dangled before them in this way, and soon one of their number, more childish and perhaps less courageous than the rest, began to shuffle forward. His was the straw hat and he wanted to get it back. He stopped for a moment but the police called to him once more, reaching out the straw hat to his hand, and the boy came on again. Then the whole group started to move slowly forward. One by one the police clapped handcuffs on their wrists and pushed them into the prison van.

Later that evening we were driving out to a dinner-party a few miles out of Johannesburg with a woman friend, and since it was still daylight and we were early I suggested we might stop on a hilltop and smoke a cigarette.

'Not here,' she said.

'Why not?'

'People get murdered here.'

'In the daylight? On a hilltop? With other cars going by?'

'Yes,' she said. 'Let's wait till we get back to the main road.'

At the dinner-party (and we had dressed in dinner jackets for it), it was the usual thing: directly the meal was over we began to play games, liar dice, poker, canasta, bridge – any sort of game so long as everyone was occupied. Such conversation as we had turned on sport (racing chiefly) and political events abroad. In the rooms the furniture was European and so were the pictures and the carpets; nothing was African. In other words, Africa was being deliberately excluded, and it had the effect of making one feel that one was on an island, that we were not merely the few rich shutting ourselves off from the many poor, but that we were white and the rest of the people around us were black. In South Africa there are still only two and a half million whites in a sea of eight or nine million coloured people, and if you take the larger area – the whole of black Africa below the bulge – the discrepancy is even greater. Then it is something like three million whites against sixty million blacks. One begins to see why Europeans in Africa make such a point of asserting their Europeanness, of wearing their formal clothes and emphasizing *their* tribal customs; it is one way of maintaining their authority and independence.

This was a theme that kept cropping up on our journey from this time onwards; this feeling of isolation among the white communities; and however placid the outward scene might have been one was always conscious of an undercurrent of uneasiness. After all, it is not so much more than sixty or seventy years since this was the dark continent and Dr Livingstone was the one white man in existence for many thousands of miles around.

I used to enjoy watching the Negroes on the roads out-side Johannesburg. They still walk in single file as though they were on a jungle path, and often one of their number will be playing a guitar or a mouth organ softly as he moves along. Then, when the moment comes for the group to split up, each man taking a different path across the fields, their conversation still continues; apparently they cannot bear to break off contact entirely and be on their own again, and so, without looking back, they keep on calling out chance after-thoughts to one another until at last their voices are lost in the distance. It all looks artless and innocent enough, a vague recapitulation of one's own childhood, of long-forgotten summer evenings when one strolled idly home from school, gossiping and playing with one's friends along the way. And yet, just because these scenes are so natural and friendly, they contain a sharp reminder to the white man that he still remains an outsider here, that *he* could never walk quite so unselfconsciously about Africa, that he is marked, in fact, by his own feeling of superiority.

It is the same thing at the mine dances on Sunday morn-ing. The audience sits in tiered seats around a sort of bull-ring, and just as in Spain, there are two kinds of seats – those in the sun and those in the shade. The Europeans sit in the shade. The miners love to dance; it is their big blow-out of the week, and in groups of a dozen or more the different tribes come in to do their turns. It is a pity of course that their traditional grass skirts and leopard skin capes should have got so mixed up with the ragged Euro-pean shirts and the aluminium miners' helmets, and that the drums should so often beat out a completely non-African tune (they were very keen on that ancient number 'I want to *be* happy/But I can't *be* happy/Till I make *you*/ Happy too'). But the true rhythm does break through quite often, the slow shuffle through the sand, the sudden blast of the leader's whistle and then the leap into the air, the fan-tastic shudderings and stampings. Then one can easily imag-ine that a lion is being hunted down and killed, that the

16

huntsmen are returning in triumph to their women in the kraal, and that some tormented ancestral spirit is being laid to rest at last. Not far from me in the sunshine a Negro spectator was busily knitting himself a pullover as he watched. He was wearing the back portion which he had already completed, and was now knitting his way, row by row, across his bare black chest in front. The needles, I noticed, kept time with the drums.

The dancers clearly were delighted that white tourists were there to watch them, but one had the strong impression that they were really dancing for themselves and their own people in the sunny stands – the true *aficionados* – and that they were responding to instincts which white men have long since regarded as much too crude and childish to be brought out and displayed like this in the open.

So much, then, for our hopes of seeing the primitive tribal life of the Africans, at any rate in the south, so we decided instead to concentrate on the principal object of our journey, the wild animals. Friends in Johannesburg willingly mapped out a route. It was to take us mainly through the great game parks that have been established within the last forty years or so, beginning with the Kruger and Hluhluwe reserves in South Africa and then taking us gradually northwards until we reached the sources of the Nile in Uganda and the Belgian Congo.

The Kruger Park, our first objective, is somewhat older and larger than most of the other game reserves. As far back as 1884 President Kruger began to take up the cause of protecting wild life in South Africa, and by the end of the century an area of 1,500 square miles had been marked off as a sanctuary on the borders of Portuguese East Africa. But it was not until 1926 that the park, with a number of large additions – it now covers 7,340 square miles, roughly the same area as Wales – really began to get under way. Its objects were commendably simple : to stop, in part at least, the wholesale slaughter of animals that was still going on, and to give both scientists and the public a chance of studying wild life in its natural surroundings. In practice, however, the policing of the park turned out to be difficult. There was no fence, of course, and the local farmers on the edge of the reserve were not easily mollified when the animals emerged at night to trample their crops and even attack their workers. Among the meat-hungry Africans who regarded all animals as their natural enemies anyway, poaching developed into a minor industry. There were such matters as forest fires, droughts, and diseases to contend with, and even the increase of the carnivora, especially the lions, presented a problem; their main prey, the ante-lopes and the zebras, began to disappear at an alarming rate at times, and some of the lions had to be shot. Even more threatening was the pressure from political groups who argued that the park lands were needed by the expanding human population for agriculture and for grazing.

It was the tourists who probably saved the day. From the first, ordinary people in Johannesburg, Durban, and other cities liked to drive out to the Kruger for a few days holiday – not to shoot, often not even to photograph, but simply to enjoy the experience of living for a little in the kind of wild surroundings which are rapidly disappearing from the earth. The money they paid in entrance fees and for their accommodation was enough to keep the project alive through its experimental years. Now in the nineteen-fifties all the original problems still exist, but it is hardly likely that the South African government will allow the park to fail. Some ninety thousand tourists passed through it in 1956, and the numbers have increased since then.

It was a lovely summer day in February when my wife and I set off by car from Johannesburg across the high veldt. The widow birds with their fantastic black tails a foot or more in length were everywhere fluttering about like pennants in the breeze. A tremendous landscape dotted with clumps of eucalyptus trees and occasional farms unfolded, and we ate a picnic lunch beside a stream. Then as we went on eastward through the afternoon we entered hot groves of semi-tropical fruits, oranges and grenadillas, pineapples and bananas. I ran over the rules of the park in

18

my mind as we drove along. No fire-arms or dogs were allowed. Once inside the entrance gate you kept below a maximum speed of twenty-five miles an hour, and if you came to a herd of elephant you stopped, turned off the engine, and waited until the last beast had gone by. Buffalo, hippopotamus, and even lion you could afford to be more casual with, and in every case you were perfectly safe, so the book instructions said, provided you remained in your car; apparently the oil and petrol fumes obliterated the human smell, and in any case the animals had grown used to cars and no longer associated them with danger. Finally, you had to be inside your fenced-in camp in the interior of the park before darkness fell, and there you remained shut in all night until the gates opened again at first light in the morning.

All this was very well in its way, and yet one wondered. What happened if the car broke down in the park before we got to the camp? Did you simply sit there all night? The book of instructions had nothing to say about this, nor did it indicate what you had to do if you lost your way along the forest tracks. What happened if you turned a corner and suddenly found yourself in a middle of a herd of elephants? Suppose too they changed course and came in your direction? It was reassuring, of course, to know that ninety thousand people had made this trip the previous year, but in the back of one's mind one remembered very vividly all the stories one had heard of big game in Africa, the ambushes, the sudden charges of the wounded buffalo. I don't think we were actually afraid; still, the conversation lapsed and we drove up to the entrance of the park very quietly in the late afternoon.

Here at least there was nothing alarming. A pole across the road. A couple of African park attendants hanging about. A white game warden in a kiosk surrounded by coloured postcards. We signed an agreement that we would do nothing to injure the animals, paid the modest fee of ten shillings a head and the same amount for the car, and then drove on. A gravelled roadway stretched directly before us into the bush, with high grass and shrubs on either side. Pretty soon we turned a corner, the kiosk vanished from the rear-view mirror, and we were on our own.

It was astonishingly quiet. We kept gazing ahead, and to either side, but nothing moved, not even a bird, and there was no sound except for the soft crunching of the tyres on the gravel. We still had five miles to go, and after a bit I accelerated a little to twenty miles an hour. Neither of us spoke. And then all at once it happened. There, not fifteen yards away, under a group of low trees stood a kudu bull. He was casually reaching up to nibble the leaves on a branch, but he stopped when he saw the car and with his moist eye full on us remained absolutely rigid. I on my side was so surprised that I stalled the engine and then hastily got it going again. And still the animal never moved. For perhaps three minutes he stood there silently gazing at us, and then with a sideways movement of his head he turned and walked away. At once a female came out of the shadows and joined him and there were sounds of other animals in the bush beyond.

I am trying to describe this incident precisely as it happened because this first sight of wild animals in their natural surroundings really is something of a revelation, and although a thousand more lively scenes may overtake the traveller later on it is the first impression which will probably remain most clearly in his mind. The colours of the animals are brighter, their outlines clearer and their eyes more sprightly, than anything one could have previously imagined. There is a kind of tense vitality in their movements, an element of challenge in their glance, that immediately diminishes you, the observer, to a much smaller stature than you thought you had before. That sense of privilege and superiority with which human beings approach another species suddenly forsakes you – you are simply another intruder in the bush on the same level as the animals themselves – and in a moment you comprehend how much human contact distorts wild creatures and destroys their proportions. While the zoo keeper forces on them an appearance that is much too soft and tame, the hunter (and incidentally the artist, the photographer, and the taxidermist too) almost invariably makes them out to be too fierce and dramatic. Few animals in a natural state spend their lives in a state of panic or rage or in violent motion. They may be constantly on the alert, but for the most part you find them simply standing there under the trees, like this kudu, quietly munching leaves; and as a spectacle it is superb.

We were lucky, of course, to have met a kudu bull at this first contact, for he is a large beast with fine spiralling horns, and he is generally conceded to be one of the noblest sights in the African bush. But it was the same with a pair of impala that bounded across in front of us a little farther down the track, the same marvellous grace and suppleness of movement; and even the unlovely baboon that met us at the gateway of the camp had a positively *soigné* air. His fur looked as though it had been freshly cleaned and brushed.

The camp where we spent the next three days was called Pretorius Kop, and has been used as a model for such camps in many of the African parks. It is a queer atmosphere. You might be living in an American motel except that here your hut is a circular affair with a thatched roof called a rondavel, and that the black boy who comes to cook your provisions calls you Bwana, and that you are deeply conscious of the fence that divides you from the surrounding bush. There is a considerable amount of come and go as the carloads of other visitors return from their evening drives around the park (they have to pay a late fee if they arrive after the gates are closed), and presently you discover that there exists here, too, as at a ski-ing chalet or even in a country golf-house, a local jargon and an expertise. One soon gets used to it. You exchange stories of the day's experiences with the other visitors, and you tend to overplay your hand a little, though in a deprecatory way, so as to keep ahead of your opponents. You call across to the people in the next rondavel who have just come in: 'See anything?'

'Nothing much. Just a few warthog and a couple of giraffe.'

Warthogs are pretty common, but the giraffe are somewhat unusual at this end of the park, and so you counter this with: 'They say there's a pride of lion up on the Sabie River road. Fellow I met saw a kill up there today.'

Hardly anyone ever sees a lion making a kill, and your neighbour now has to think fast if he is going to go one better. Possibly he will make some such remark as: 'Yes, I know about those lion. I got within ten yards of them yesterday.' Or perhaps, 'You didn't miss the wildebeest and the zebra on the Skukuza track, did you? There must have been a hundred of them there this morning.'

And so on.

Then too, there is a certain *cachet* in having visited the other game parks as well – and usually any park is better than the one you are actually in. 'You can't see much here in the summer,' we were told, 'the grass is too high. If you want elephant – and they're the best of the lot – you have to go up to the Wankie in Southern Rhodesia. I suppose we must have run into a couple of hundred of them there last year.' Or again: 'Well, of course if you haven't seen the White Rhino down at Hluhluwe you haven't seen anything yet. They're dangerous too.'

This is the point. Danger, or at any rate the illusion of it, seems to be required to give a sparkle to the visitor's curiosity, and he is constantly being reminded by the authorities that, despite the matter of fact way in which he is allowed to drive about for quite long distances on his own, a danger does exist. At Pretorious Kop notices warn you in Africaans: *'Bly in die pad. Bly in u kar. Spoedbeperking 25 m.p.u.'* 'Keep to the road. Stay in your car. Speed limit 25 m.p.h.' And more explicitly: *'Olifante is gevaarlik. Pasop!'* 'Elephants are dangerous. Keep your distance!'

Gladly at first you keep your distance. You are not reassured by the photographs showing lions crouching on the bonnets of cars and peering placidly through the windscreen at the occupants inside, nor by the fact that they

22

will sometimes walk alongside the traffic on the roads, using it as a screen to approach their quarry. You are indignant at the fools who occasionally will drive up to a lioness resting with her cubs in the midday heat beside the track and throw beer-bottles to stir her up. On this first night when all is quiet within the camp you sit on the porch of your rondavel, and you hear – or think you hear – some distant roar in the jungle, some night-bird brushing past in the sky, and you are overtaken with a quite genuine sense of adventure and excitement. And in the morning with the first white light of dawn you drive out very cautiously to see what you can see.

Often for quite long periods nothing happens. You drive up hopefully to each corner, and still the empty silent scrub expands before you. But there is always another corner ahead, and so you keep going and you make a virtue out of the fact that at least you have seen a lilac-breasted roller perched on a tree stump and the tracks of some large animal around a water-hole. In this way perhaps half an hour goes by, and like a disappointed fisherman you feel your sense of expectancy gradually draining away. Then when the animals do appear – and sometimes they fairly crowd upon you, as many as half a dozen species feeding together – you experience an almost childish glow of satisfaction. You stop the car, automatically you talk in whispers as you get your field-glasses into focus. Even though the herd may be barely thirty or forty yards away it is only gradually that the individual animals insinuate themselves into your view among the patches of shade and sunlight, and it is not until you have looked again a second and a third time that you become aware of a group of waterbuck on the left, the sprinkling of impala among the zebras, and the bright beady eye of some small cat-like creature surveying you from the branches overhead. Despite the general air of watchfulness the animals give the impression that they have been quietly grazing there for a long time, and as a rule nothing very dramatic occurs. The outlying members of the herd look up sharply when you first arrive, move off a little way into the scrub, and then begin grazing again.

The things that really startle them – the whiff of a hunting lion in the long grass, the warning flight of some bird above their heads – are usually too subtle for you to notice. All you are aware of is a sudden unnatural stillness in the bush. Every head has been jerked erect and turned in the same direction, every animal has frozen into the rigidity of a statue. For perhaps a minute or two they remain like this, and then, apparently reassured, they relax again. At other times the herd is seized with an ungovernable panic, and in a second the peaceful pattern is shattered by a wild commotion, the guinea fowl scuttling into the undergrowth, the zebra running together in a pack with their tails flying out behind them, the antelopes every ten yards or so making immense jumps into the air in the hope of catching a brief glimpse of the approaching enemy; and in a moment you are entirely alone in the clearing.

After a day or two of this one begins to realize that one must reassemble one's ideas about the wild animals in Africa. Somewhere in the tangled background of one's education something seems to have gone wrong; and now it is not the strangeness of the things that one is seeing that is so impressive – it is their false familiarity. Like most of our generation (the lost one dating back to before the First World War) my wife and I had grown up with the legend of Africa, the danger-legend of the explorer and the white hunter, of Rider Haggard's tales and many a movie star on safari. The lion springs, the elephant charges with a terrifying bellow, and it is always some poor human devil who is going to get the worst of it unless he shoots quick.

Here in the Kruger Park, however, we were confronted with something quite different, the legend, as it were, within the legend: the animals reacting not to human beings but to themselves and to the surrounding forest. In other words, once you remove the human element – and in particular the emphasis on human danger – an entirely new world emerges. You see that an elaborate and subtle skein

24

of influences is at work; that, for instance, there was a very good reason why those zebra and impala and other antelopes should have been grazing together; one species excels in hearing, another in smell, and another in sight, and together they establish a very effective warning system against their common enemies, the lions, the leopards, and other carnivora.

These discoveries tend to create in one a simple unaffected pleasure. It is, of course, an obvious escape-entertainment, but there is nothing really synthetic about it because one quickly realizes, however calcified and disillusioned one may be, that this is a world that we knew very well when we were young; the dream world of the jungle stories to which we listened in a trance of sympathy and fear and quite definitely *wanted* to believe. And although this world has nothing to do with human beings it is often more moving, more entertaining, and much more terrible than anything which has been dreamed of in the movies or the sportsmen's notebooks.

I found myself especially attracted to some of the lesser species, mostly I suppose because nobody had ever bothered to tell me about them before. Who, for example, ever writes about the warthog? Yet you find him everywhere in this part of Africa; he has a small trotting-on part in every other scene. The warthog is the clown of the jungle, and he has a certain awful charm. He is an extremely bothered animal about the size of a small pig, and he is furnished with two enormous tusks, a lion's mane, and a tail and hindquarters which are quite uncompromisingly bare. He roots about the ground in family groups, and if surprised he stands and stares for a moment with deep concern written all over his appalling face. Then with a flick of his head, his tail rising like a railway signal bolt upright behind him, the father of the group is off into the scrub. The rest of the family follow in line, the biggest first and the smallest drawing up frantically in the rear. The warthog is not really ugly – it is the sort of countenance that is covered roughly by the French phrase '*une jolie laide'*, yet by his mere appearance he has been known to stampede a herd of buffalo.

There were a lot of warthogs around Pretorius Kop while we were there, and we were told that they had a passion for a little wild green apple called a Marula that falls to the ground in summer. In this African heat the fruit ferments quickly and the warthogs sometimes become quite drunk. Instead of bolting in the usual way they stand and gaze at the intruder with a bemused and careless eye. Then the instinct for self-preservation dimly asserts itself, and they turn and make a befuddled rush for a few yards, stop, change direction, and then plunge off again. Finally they subside to sleep on the ground to awake to heaven knows what sort of primeval hangover in the morning.

With the giraffe, at the other end of the scale, much the tallest creature in the bush, it is quite different. Here is the least demonstrative of animals (it has no vocal cords and utters only the smallest of sounds, a sort of sighing snort in the throat), and in all Africa it is certainly the most decorative thing alive. We came on a family one day in the Kruger Park – just the two parents and one half-grown child – and for a long time, with their heads thrown slightly back, they surveyed us across the tops of the acacia trees. Giraffes have a slightly affronted air when they are disturbed; somehow they contrive to make you feel as though you have just said something in particularly bad taste, and they sniff the breeze reproachfully. The skins of this group were superb : smooth and bright and glossy, so bright indeed that they stood out plainly against the bush, as plainly as the stripes of the zebras do. Clearly this pattern of jagged brown squares is meant to camouflage the animal by breaking up its outline, but it didn't seem to be very effective at a range of thirty yards; not, at any rate, with those ten-foot necks swaying above us like vast asparagus stalks among the trees. And then abruptly they were off. No living creature in this world runs as the giraffe does. It moves its legs in pair on either side, first the right side forward then the left, and this imparts a singular undulating motion to the huge beast. It flows across the countryside with the delayed rhythm of a film in slow motion, and it is perfectly wonderful to watch.

Later on, in other parts of Africa, we saw many giraffes and learned a lot about them, and it was always something rather pleasant and outlandish. In parts of Kenya, for example, they have had to raise the telephone lines a clear six feet or so to allow the big bulls (they grow to seventeen or eighteen feet) to pass beneath; and at Hluhluwe there was the strange story of the giraffe who simply could not believe in itself. It was a baby just a few days old that had been abandoned by its mother (possibly because she had had two offspring and could not feed both), and a farmer had picked it up and brought it to the game warden's house. For three and a half years the warden looked after the orphan; it was brought up with his own children and played with them every day. When it grew too big to come into the house it kept mooning through the windows at the warden and his family while they were eating dinner, and it followed them around to their bedrooms through the garden when they went to bed. Finally it was decided that the moment had come when the animal, now fully grown, should join his own kind, and he was taken off to a herd of wild giraffe that had recently come into the park. But one look was sufficient. The small brain was quite unable to register the fact that such extraordinary animals could exist, and that he was one of them : he turned and bolted. They took him back half a dozen times with the same result, and in the end they gave it up. A little lonely and reproachful, the tame giraffe lives now in a specially constructed paddock near the warden's house.

All the animals in the parks are of course in the process of adapting themselves to human beings, and an uneven but quite definite evolution is being observed as the years go by. At Kruger Park birds still cannot always estimate the speed of approaching cars, and they occasionally smash themselves into the wind-screens. Sometimes herds of impala (those charming small antelopes with lyre-shaped horns that are impossible to dissociate from Walt Disney's Bambi) are seized with the frantic desire to stampede at the sight of a vehicle on the road. One animal with a mighty bound into the air starts it, and the others follow. The leaders get across the road safely, but the others coming on behind, their vision obscured by dust, are likely to crash into you. Giraffes too will sometimes rush blindly forward in this way, and one kick from that tremendous fore-leg can smash the radiator of a car.

On the other hand, elephants and some of the larger carnivora have quickly got to know the limits of the park, and they realize they are safe from human interference there. If they stray over the borders at night into the neighbouring farms in search of food they take good care to be back again inside the park before morning breaks.

There is, in fact, a constant noctural warfare going on along the frontiers of every park, the animals going out and the poachers coming in. African game rangers armed with rifles and posted every quarter of a mile or so along the more populated boundaries of the Kruger Park do a certain amount towards keeping the situation under control, but they are not always effective; it grows lonely on your own in the bush, there is an immense temptation for a man to try a bottle or two of the local home-brewed beer, and after that to sleep. And while he sleeps the poachers come creeping in with their spears and wire snares.

I had imagined that it might be an exciting experience to drive about the park at night, that the bush then became alive with staring eyes, and that all sorts of horrendous shrieks and cries resounded in the undergrowth; but the game rangers told me it was not a bit like this. One rarely saw or heard anything at all. Just occasionally, they said, some of the smaller beasts would dart across the road or an antelope of some kind would become transfixed in the headlights. The impala were very easy to catch in this way; they simply stood there, utterly demoralized, gazing into the lights, and you could walk up and grab them by the horns.

For my part, I felt very little desire to break the rules

and sally out of the camp at night. More than once when we were returning at sunset from some outlying part my wife and I debated what we would do if the car broke down. We agreed that if it were only a matter of a mile or two back to camp we would walk and risk it; further than that, no, we would wait until morning.

It was absurd of course. In Africa pythons don't drop on you out of trees, and it is only by the most random accident that a man will be trampled by an elephant or attacked by a hungry lion at night. But nothing will stop the imagination working. One looks at these rolling endless hills of scrub as the night closes in, one pictures oneself lost out there in the blackness, and at once one recognizes the characters in the Ancient Mariner's vision:

> Like one that on a lonesome road
> Doth walk in fear and dread,
> And having once turned round, walks on,
> And turns no more his head;
> Because he knows a fearful fiend
> Doth close behind him tread.

The man on the lonesome road is you, lost in the park, and the fearful fiend is a leopard lying in wait in the branches above your head.

These visions had a powerful influence on one unlucky visitor to Pretorius Kop, not long ago. This man was driving alone, and by some mischance, just as night was falling, he turned down a side track which had been closed to visitors because the bridges along it had been washed away. Darkness still found him wandering about, and in something of a panic he rushed at one of the little streams in his path. Half-way across the engine flooded and would not start again. With the water flowing just an inch or two below the floorboards he waited there all night. The game warden at the gate was only a couple of miles away, but even in the morning the man still did not care to walk. He waited in his car all through the day and the next night, and it was only by chance that an African park attendant came bicycling down the deserted track on the second morning. He found the man in a state of mild hysteria, and it was some little time before he could be induced to get out of his car and wade over to the bank.

There have been very few incidents in the history of the Kruger Park to justify such extreme fear. Game rangers do get mauled by lions from time to time; occasionally a female elephant that has been separated from her young will make a charge, but the truth of the matter is that large wild animals will not usually attack human beings. Their instinct is to escape from men whenever they see them, and, with odd exceptions, it is only when they have been hunted and wounded that they become dangerous.

'In the old days,' one veteran sportsman told me, 'rhino, buffalo, and elephant always used to charge, but that was because we were always out shooting them. I have still never seen a rhino in any other position except coming at me head on. It is only recently and only in the game reserves that the animals have become relatively tame.' And he went on to speak of a kind of glee for killing which used to possess the early settlers in South Africa; just to see an animal was enough, they *had* to kill it. He remembered one farmer telling him with delight how just that day he had succeeded with five shots in wiping out the last five survivors of a rare species of antelope.

And so an endless spiral is created: the huntsman – the native with the poisoned arrow, the sportsman with the rifle – deliberately creates danger for himself by attacking the animals, and this danger, this created risk, then becomes the justification for his hunting.

At Kruger Park they tell a story of a noted game warden named Wolhuter, who was clawed from his horse by two lions one day, and although terribly mauled managed to survive. Wolhuter's son is now a ranger at the Kruger Park, and he continues to ride on horseback. 'My father had bad luck,' he told me. 'Nine times out of ten no lion will molest you even if it's hungry. Sometimes the younger lions – the two- and three-year-olds – will chase a man on horseback but they only do it for fun, and you can easily get away. Whenever we have had a serious case it has always been because the animal has been in pain. I remember not long ago an African game ranger was knocked off his bicycle by a lion and killed. Afterwards when the animal was shot it was found to be in agony from a thorn in its foot. But that was a very rare case.'

After three days at Pretorius Kop my wife and I turned south to Hluhluwe (Sushloo-wee is about the nearest I can get to the correct pronunciation) in the hope of catching a glimpse of the rare and allegedly dangerous white rhinoceros. This involved a journey of some hundreds of miles through the British protectorate of Swaziland. Swaziland is the Rider Haggard country; these are the hills that Allan Quatermain and his friends trudged across in search of King Solomon's Mines. At Mbabane (another phonetical snare – Imbarbarn seems to be the local usage) the proprietress of our hotel took me out on to the veranda one evening and pointed to the west. 'Look,' she said, 'Queen Sheba's Breasts.' There they were, two pointed peaks on the skyline, just as Haggard had described them, and the track that wound down through the pass was obviously the track that Quatermain had followed.

The rest of Swaziland, a green and lovely countryside, was almost as romantic. We called on Sohhuze, the reigning chief, a man who speaks English but lives in a kraal of native huts and on occasion receives visitors mounted on the back of a warrior. He was unable to see us, however; a polite message was sent out saying that the country was suffering from drought and that he was making rain.

It fell that night – four inches, to be exact – and it turned half Swaziland into a quagmire of impassable black mud. It was in the tail end of this cloudburst that we drove down to the shores of the Indian Ocean and thence to the Hluhluwe reserve in Natal.

At Hluhluwe, a much smaller park than Kruger, the main camp of thatched huts perches on a ridge. You see it from a long way off, but the last few miles are rather difficult going on a steep and winding road; and it was here that our car burnt out a coil and came to a dead stop. Two days of thrashing about in the Swaziland mud had been too much for it. There was still half an hour of daylight to go, and since the camp was just above us we decided to walk. As it so often happens, however, we underestimated the distance and the sun set very quickly. I don't think that either of us were very disturbed about the animals at that moment; we were too tired and dishevelled at the end of the long day, and we would probably have reached the camp without giving them a thought had not some people driven up behind us. They asked: 'Aren't you frightened to walk at night with the rhino about?' The white rhinoceros! He was beginning to sound like the white whale in Melville's *Moby Dick*, and certainly we would have been frightened had we remembered him.

Next day, however, when we went to see the huge beasts it turned out that the white rhinoceros is hardly dangerous at all, not at any rate as rhinoceroses go. The African ranger who was with us calmly got out of the car we had borrowed and walked up to a group of half a dozen of them. We followed gingerly, choosing a path along a line of easily climbable trees; and there they stood, not twenty yards away. As far as I could see they were like any other rhinoceros except that the colour of their hides was dirty grey. They mooned about through the bush with a fine antediluvian deliberation, and although they were perfectly well aware of our presence – a rhinoceros has very bad eyesight but its sense of smell is acute – they seemed to be neither annoyed nor surprised.

It is the ordinary black rhinoceros that is dangerous, and when on the following day we came on a large female with its young our guide would by no means allow us to get out of the car. Instead he instructed me to keep the engine running and be ready to move off at speed. The black species (it is actually light orange in colour when it has been rolling in the mud, a thing it often does) is the most unpredictable of African animals. Occasionally it will charge a car, and nearly always it will go for a man on foot if he approaches too close. With over a ton weight coming at you at twenty miles an hour you don't stand much of a chance. Among themselves the rhinoceroses are constantly fighting, the females included, and it is not the two horns, the front one perhaps three feet long and sharply pointed, which do the damage; it is the terrific lunging blow delivered by the animal's shoulder. This sets up internal injuries in his opponent. The black rhinoceros, in fact, very well establishes the point made by the late Bernard Shaw that carnivora (lions, tigers, leopards, and many human beings) tend to skulk and turn away at the sign of danger, while vegetarians (bulls, rhinoceroses, buffaloes, and Shaw himself) are much more belligerent.

At Hluhluwe we heard much argument about how these and other large wild animals which have always been regarded as the prerogative of the hunter are going to be preserved. Once you have got them into the park do you allow nature to take its course and achieve its own balance? Or do you shoot off a few lions, leopards, and cheetah when you find that they are making too much havoc among the lesser game? Do you burn off the grass each year to bring on the new spring growth, or again do you let the natural vegetable process have its own way? These and other technical questions, we discovered, are debated all the way up and down East Africa, and there does not appear to be any general agreement in sight. Each park makes its own rules.

But it is the question of disease which is the really dominant issue. Wild animals, though not usually affected themselves, are carriers of a parasite called Trypanosome, which is spread by the tsetse fly. It is disastrous both to cattle and to human beings (it carries sleeping sickness) and there are other plagues which they also help to spread. Until recently the usual remedy was simple: exterminate the wild animals. The slaughter was fantastic and was not confined to Africa. In 1924, for example, there was an outbreak of foot and mouth disease in the Stanislaus National Park in the United States. Some 22,000 deer were shot, and both disease and animals were exterminated together. In Zululand, close to the Hluhluwe, there was a much more drastic affair in the nineteen-forties. Nagana, the tsetse fly disease, took hold, and a systematic destruction of all wild animals began. Between 1942 and 1950 138,329 head of big game were shot. And still the disease was not stamped out.

Nowadays more imaginative methods are being tried: spraying from the air is one answer, and in some places the tsetse fly is kept back by lopping the foliage of the bigger shrubs. But these are expensive experiments, and it is still general practice for governments in Africa to order the destruction of large numbers of game whenever disease threatens a settled area. Only in such remote places as the Kalahari desert in Bechuanaland are the animals really safe – at all events for the next few decades. Here in the Kalahari, where the only roads are the dried-up courses of rivers that flow just once or twice a century, vast herds of gemsbok (an antelope with a white blazed face and two horns like spears) roam about; and the lion, the kudu, and the springbok are still left pretty much to themselves. In the Gemsbok Park the only human inhabitants are those lamentable bushmen, some forty of them in all, who do nothing but lie in the sun all day.

As for the other parks, it seems to be everywhere agreed that they will all have to be fenced off one day if they are going to survive, a vast project requiring millions upon millions of pounds. Up-to-date fencing has only been tried out on a small scale in South Africa to protect the Addo elephants, a special breed that lives in an impenetrable jungle near Port Elizabeth. These elephants used to trespass on the citrus fruit farms nearby, and they were shot at until only eleven beasts were left. Then the government stepped in and constructed a fence of tramlines and lift cables, eleven and a half miles in length, its posts sunk six feet into the ground; and behind this barrier the elephants have slowly begun to breed again.

At Hluhluwe, however, one is not much aware of any of

these problems. Poaching seems to be at a minimum, and there are no lions to eat the smaller beasts or elephants to trample the neighbouring farms. It is the prettiest park in Africa. During the long wet summer it blooms with such flowering trees as flamboyants, frangipani, and mimosa, and there is a refreshing greenness everywhere. Unlike the Kruger Park where, for the most part, you drive along bush tracks on a level with animals, here the ground is broken up into small hills and valleys; and since the roads run along the ridges you look down on the game from above and see them not individually but in herds and in constant movement. In one short early morning drive we saw rhinoceros, buffalo, wildebeest, nyala (an antelope which is distinguished, in the male, by a coat of gunmetal blue with an unusually bright white stripe down the back), warthog, impala, baboons, monkeys, zebra, and one solitary ostrich: quite a bag to mention casually to our neighbours in the next rondavel when we got back. An ostrich seen close-to in the bush looks like nothing so much as a preposterously enlarged chicken, and there is something a little indecent about its huge bare legs. I had been told that ostriches sometimes swallow stones and pebbles as an aid to digestion, and unless I am much mistaken our specimen was doing precisely that. He was pecking at a patch of gravel when we came by, and I saw him raise his tiny head and gulp awkwardly a couple of times before he paced away. Incidentally, it is quite untrue that ostriches bury their heads in the sand at the approach of danger. They may bend their necks down to the ground, but they do this so that they will not be seen from far off across the plain.

In Hluhluwe too we first began to observe the storks. They come down here to the Cape of Good Hope in great flocks around October every year, and then at the end of February begin to assemble for their long six-thousand mile flight back to Europe. This is a delightful thing to see. Just a few birds appear in the sky one day, slowly spiralling around, and from hour to hour newcomers add to their numbers. Then again on the following day still more storks arrive to join the slow circle in the sky, and the same process may go on for a week or more. Finally all the members of this particular flock are gathered together; by some mysterious means the signal for the start is given and in mass formation they wheel away to the north. April and May find them repairing their crude nests of sticks on the cottage chimneypots in Alsace-Lorraine and Holland. Just a few of the older and the weaker birds don't feel equal to this journey, and often, I was told, you will see them loitering about in the swamps and the marshes in South Africa through the winter, like elderly holiday-makers who linger on in half-deserted seaside hotels long after the season is over.

CHAPTER TWO

THE HYRAX IN ARCADIA

CENTRAL AFRICA – the part that takes in the Belgian Congo, Uganda, Kenya, Tanganyika, and the new Federation of Rhodesia – still remains, by some way, the most African part of the whole continent. In the south the European influence is very strong, and the north (if you except the deserts) really belongs to the Mediterranean and the Middle East. But here in the centre you experience a strong sense of isolation; and even the more obvious tourist haunts like the Victoria Falls and Kilimanjaro are still insulated from the outside world by a wilderness of virtually empty plains. This region is also wonderful country for wild game. During the rains which fall usually from the end of March until June and then again from October until the end of December the animals scatter away from the lakes and rivers, but they return again as soon as the dry weather sets in, and that is the time to go and see them.

Travelling is not particularly difficult. In the last twenty years or so a network of roads has been pushed into the interior, and you can usually find a hotel or a camp of some sort at the end of the day's run. The heat is not oppressive – most of the time you are travelling 3,000 feet or more above the level of the sea – and the Africans everywhere have long since grown used to strangers.

My wife and I in our journey northwards from the game parks of South Africa approached this huge area (it is roughly the size of Europe) by way of Livingstone in Southern Rhodesia. We hoped to see something of the elephants in the Wankie reserve, which lies a little to the west of the town, and we flew up there from Johannesburg one Sunday morning. But now we were beaten by the weather. Great rainstorms had made the roads impassable, and although we did manage to get into one corner of the park and see a few sable (the antelope with the splendid backward curving horns), most of the other animals had left the water holes and scattered into the bush. The droppings of elephant were everywhere, and so too were the trees they had knocked down in order to get the berries and succulent green leaves at the top. But there were no elephant. And so we turned back to the main attraction of the district – the Victoria Falls.

It is a little difficult at first to get your bearings in this strange place because the falling water disappears abruptly into a slit in the earth's surface, and thereafter the river, the Zambezi, rushes away along a narrow gorge that keeps twisting and turning back on itself in the most confusing way. Consequently from ground level it is impossible to obtain a general view. The thing that really takes your eye, however, is a white cloud that constantly hangs over the scene. From the distance this cloud looks like a forest fire (the native name for the falls is Musi-o-tunya, the Smoke that Thunders), but in actual fact it is composed of tiny particles of water which have been carried into the sky by the displaced air rushing from the bottom of the gorge. If you stand on the edge of the falls themselves you feel this cool wet updraught-very keenly, and it is rather like being in the midst of a fine scotch mist, except that the sun shines through and creates astonishing circular rainbows in the air. In the midday heat condensation sets in and the cloud diminishes, but in the evening and in the early mornings it climbs up to a thousand feet again.

The Zambezi does not hasten to the falls. It slides, flat, blue-grey, and placid, among islands across the plain, and then unexpectedly plunges headlong into the vast abyss. Sometimes hippopotami, grown feeble with sickness or badly wounded in one of their communal fights, are washed helplessly over the lip, and then for weeks on end their bodies float round and round in the whirlpools in the chasm below. No one has yet succeeded in plumbing these depths; even a cable weighted with a steel rail is swept out at a tangent by the torrent. Crocodiles take good care to remain in the calm water above the falls, and though it is not often you see them they are always there. A notice on the bank states with simple emphasis: 'Swimming is suicidal.'

Apart from this and a few other unobtrusive signs of the white man's civilization, the falls remain pretty much as they were when Dr Livingstone discovered them on 16 November 1855. The same bulging baobab trees that Livingstone described grow along the bank, the same orchids thrust up through the dank and rotten undergrowth, and precisely in July each year the elephants still return from the dry wastes of Bechuanaland looking for water. The river then is low, and they wade out to King George Island washing themselves as they go along with an inexpressible satisfaction.

Livingstone's spirit broods very much over this country; they have an excellent collection of his maps and letters in the town, and here at the falls a lifelike statue has been erected. The doctor gazes steadfastly at the rushing water, his bible and his field-glasses in his left hand, his walking stick in his right, his cap with flaps on his head, his trousers caught up by string around his shins, and in the evening light one can easily imagine that it is the great man himself who is standing there, and that nothing much divides you from his century-old loneliness and his utter determination.

A curious sort of mesmerism is created by so much roaring, tumbling water. If you stare at it long enough you have the feeling that you are being gently lifted from the earth. You float in a solitary detachment, and it is not unpleasant. Nothing seems to be of much importance, except that this pattern should go on constantly repeating itself, that these millions of tons of water should keep on arriving, poising for a moment as they inevitably spill over the brink, and then vanish into the depths below. One can understand the morbid attraction waterfalls have for people about to commit suicide – and such tragedies do occur here from time to time. These people avoid the prospect of a horrible death among the crocodiles upstream; they want to fall with the water. Often it has a soothing effect, making them behave right up to the end in the most matter of fact way. Quite recently, I was told, a woman came up to a man who was standing on the brink and said to him casually, 'Would you mind holding my handbag for a minute?' He took the bag and then she jumped.

Then too there are the accidents. No railings have been erected above the gorge, and at many places foolhardy people like to clamber down among the wet rocks to get a closer view. If they slip, their only chance of survival lies in being caught by the clumps of trees that grow out from the face of the precipice. This happened to a man not long ago, and although the fire brigade played its searchlights about all night they could not find him. It was only by chance that in the morning a tourist happened to see a tiny figure far below clinging to a ledge. The man was beating dementedly on the rock in a futile attempt to be heard above the roaring water. They went down with ropes and ladders and got him to the top.

Normally of course the atmosphere of Livingstone is a great deal more cheerful than this. As at Niagara, honeymoon couples arrive. Launches ply about among the hippopotami on the upper reaches of the river, and native boys push the tourists in toy railway cars between the hotel and the falls. Monkeys come down from the trees to snatch cake from the picnic parties on the islands, and baboons, with great acumen, have learned how to open car doors and windows when the owners are away. There is an orchestra playing on the hotel terrace in the evening when for a few short minutes the white cloud reflects the colours of the sunset; and in the morning, at dawn, one can take a joy-ride in a plane as far as the Wankie reserve and back to the falls again. In short, it is the immemorial pattern of any beauty spot in any country, but set into an African background; and this is not a background that quite accepts the western world as yet. One is very conscious of the fact that outside this little half-formed circle of civilization the vast uninhabited bush stretches away: 'Miles and miles of bloody Africa,' is the local settlers' way of describing it.

It can be a little disturbing at times, this emptiness, this absence of every familiar thing with which one has grown up. Even in the best of circumstances it needs a certain amount of stamina to travel through Africa. Dust and heat (or else mud and storms) are likely to be with you every day. Often, if you are constantly on the move, you reach a saturation point in sightseeing where the human brain refuses to respond to new stimuli any more, and it is not always easy to relax. Africa still surrounds you. The mosquito hovers over the bed at night and the same relentless sun comes up again in the morning.

It was interesting watching the non-African tourists arriving at the falls. Many of them were middle-aged or elderly people from Europe or America (the women in sun-suits, the men in shorts and panama hats), who clearly had planned this journey long in advance and had perhaps saved up for it through many years. They travelled in organized groups of perhaps three or four carloads, and they were making their way from the Cape of Good Hope as far north as Uganda and the Belgian Congo. Some indeed were embarked on voyages round the world, and were taking in this slice of Africa merely as a sideshow. They had very little time – a certain number of miles had to be covered every day – and consequently they sometimes looked a little jaded. Too much was happening to them too quickly, and although they were gathering experiences which they would relate with pleasure when they got home, they were really more interested, by the time they got to Victoria Falls, in the food that was being provided for them (not always very good in Africa), in the absence of such comforts as iced water, and in the idiosyncrasies of their fellow-travellers.

'I want it to be understood,' I heard one woman saying at the hotel reception desk, 'that I am not going to share a room with Mrs Robertson any more. I've had her for ten days. I want to be alone.' In the bar there was another globetrotter who had been rushed through a dozen game reserves in a row. 'As far as I'm concerned,' he said wearily, 'if you've seen one hippopotamus you've seen the lot.'

Then there was the man who had developed his own peculiar method of coping with the ennui of travelling round the world. He had a patience board which was provided with little slots where the cards could be held in position if he was interrupted in the middle of the game. He had played patience steadily on a long journey that had already taken him through Japan and south-east Asia and he was playing it now. He had the board conveyed to his bedroom in the hotel, and there he sat until it was time for his party to move on again. He did not visit the falls.

These people were not bad-tempered or even particularly disillusioned. They were tired. For the moment they had had enough. The realization of their dreams of travelling through the African wilds had arrived perhaps a little too late in life.

For my wife and myself, however, still in the early stage of our journey, it was quite different. We flew on to Kenya, eager to see more, and there, using Nairobi as a base, we made a number of excursions that took us westward to Uganda and the Congo, southwards into Tanganyika, and northward almost as far as the Abyssinian border.

Before setting out on each trip we used to spend at least one evening at the Nairobi National Park – a thing that every visitor to Nairobi is practically bound to do. There is nothing quite like this place in the rest of Africa. It covers only forty square miles, but it reveals the whole world of wild game, as it were, in miniature; it is a sort of curtain-raiser to all the wider and wilder scenes you are going to see on your safari. The park, moreover, lies so close to Nairobi that the hyenas are said to come scavenging through the city streets at night. All you do is to take a taxi from your hotel and in a quarter of an hour or so you are at the gates.

The hour before dusk is the best time to arrive, and the sunset colours then can be quite wonderful. For the most part the park is rolling grassland dotted with flat-topped acacia trees, and consequently every living thing that moves is instantly revealed. We ourselves, on our first visit to the Park, had not been five minutes inside the gate before a lioness got up beside us on the road. She strolled across to a commanding rock and squatted on her haunches there, a brown silhouette in the evening light. Everything about a lion in its wild state is immediately recognizable from your own domestic cat; it has the same soft delayed tread across the grass, the same quick turning of its head to lick the fur on its shoulder, the twitching tail, the same terrible indifference. This lioness was a perfect specimen. There she sat on the rock ten yards above us, absolutely motionless, half cat and half statue of a cat, and all around her herds of gazelle and wildebeest, of zebra and impala, were quietly grazing. A line of ostriches passed by on the skyline, and on the slopes below a score of baboons of assorted sizes were scratching mechanically. But the lioness was not hunting. She simply sat and watched, and perhaps made observations which would come in useful on another, hungrier day.

In the distance we could see that half a dozen cars filled with other visitors had gathered in a circle at the bottom of a water-course and we bumped over the rocks towards them. There in the long grass, at a distance of about twelve feet, two other lionesses and eight cubs were playing. This is the kind of scene which has made Nairobi Park famous, and it is scarcely credible that one can get so close. Both mothers were lying on their backs with their paws in the air, and the cubs were pretending to fight them. The younger ones were not very clever at this game; they came stalking through the long grass with great intentness, but just as they were about to pounce something would distract their attention – a butterfly passing by on the breeze, another cub stealing up behind them – and then they would prance on their hind legs making wild swipes in the air or tumbling over one another on the ground. Their heavy heads seemed at times just a bit too heavy for them to handle, and often their weak legs got hopelessly out of control. The older cubs, however, were much more professional; although it would be another year or more before their mothers had taught them how to go out and kill for themselves, that quick growling pounce to the throat was entirely realistic. Once or twice, when the game grew too rough, the mother would bare her teeth a little and with one lazy calculated blow the cub would be sent tumbling head over heels into the grass.

We watched for an hour. Then at last when the daylight was fading one of the lionesses got up and began to walk slowly along the rocky floor of the valley. Three or four cubs came gambolling behind her, but the other mother with a low throaty grunt, almost a cough, called them back; and after a moment of protest they came. There can be nothing quite so noble as the sight of a lioness going off like this in the dusk to hunt. She paces along with her head down and with an air of absolute certainty and authority. She knows that there is no other beast – not even the elephant or the buffalo – that would normally dare to attack her, and that the whole forest waits in fear as she passes by. One thinks with pity of the smaller animals – the baby zebras, for example. They look like something out of a toy shop, a rocking horse perhaps; a new kind of rocking horse with stripes. And yet one longs to see the kill.

However, on this night the darkness closed in and this particular lioness vanished into the rocks. No doubt before morning she would kill an animal large enough for both families to eat.

There is, of course, no end of lion lore in Africa, and everyone has some sort of a lion story to tell. Yet they are not very hardy animals, at all events when they are young. They tend to get rickets, and it is not exceptional for two out of a litter of three to die. One of the game wardens gave me an example of this. He said he had seen a lioness make a kill, and without leaving the victim she grunted softly towards a clump of bushes close by. At once three cubs emerged and came over to the meal. But still the mother did not eat. She grunted again, listened, and grunted a third time. When there was still no response she got up impatiently and plucked out of the bushes a fourth cub that was apparently too weak to walk. She held the tiny beast very delicately in her jaws, and returning to the carcass dumped it on to the meat.

Once the lion is full grown his chances of survival are probably better than those of most other animals, for he has no enemy except mankind. Until extreme old age he has good hearing, sight, and smell, is an excellent swimmer and can climb trees. Around fifteen he dies.

As we went back towards the park gate that evening I saw that one of the first flocks of storks had already arrived on its northward journey to Europe. The birds were restless. They kept landing and taking off again. But presently by some communal instinct they chose a group of acacia trees and finally settled down there for the night.

It is the nearness of these things at the Nairobi Park that is so astonishing, the strange conjunction of the city a quarter of an hour away and the lioness somewhere out there in the open launching herself for the kill. One feels as though one had been to a drive-in cinema, and that now that the show is over the animals, like actors, ought to vanish from the stage until it is time for them to perform again in the morning.

We set out by car for Kisumu on Lake Victoria on the following day. For the first few miles outside Nairobi the road ran north over a countryside of bright green farms, and then abruptly it plunged down into the Great Rift Valley. This is the trough that extends all the way to the Dead Sea in the Middle East, and as a lesson in elementary geology hardly anything could be so clear; it really does look as though a great slice of the earth has dropped like an elevator on to another floor. We ran along the valley for an hour or two and then climbed out of it again towards the Aberdare mountains. Mount Kenya lay over on the right, a peak of 17,000 feet which stands fairly on the Equator and is forever under snow. Only bamboo forests grow up there on the higher slopes, and they are said to be inhabited by stray elephants that have somehow learned to withstand the extreme cold.

All this area is known as the White Highlands, and it was once notorious for the escapades of a hard-drinking group of settlers who came out from England in the nineteen-twenties and thirties. These were the 'cheque-book farmers', and from all accounts it was a pretty lively existence, an attempt to combine the elegance of the south of France and Mayfair with the wildness of Africa. All too often the champagne parties ended with quarrels over runaway wives and shooting affrays in the morning; and since so many of these people came from well-known families they provided a useful source of news for the more sensational press in England. Things culminated in the murder of the Earl of Errol in 1941, and after that the war closed in and put a stop to the more lurid escapades, possibly for ever. Nowadays the White Highlands is a very sober place of farms and cattle ranching, and the local place-names – Happy Valley, Blood Pressure Ridge – have a slightly dated sound.

Outwardly the country is very much as one has heard it described: the wide plains with the mountains in the distance: the townships which very neatly reveal the uneasy three-sided life of Kenya. Up on the hill is the English colony with its lawns and tennis-courts and bungalows. Down in the main street of the town is the shopping bazaar which is run almost entirely by Indians. Out in the slums and in the plains beyond the city limits live the Africans, and they seem to be forever on the move. They march like ants, in long processions, nearly always in single file, and every woman is bound to have some object poised on her head, a bunch of bananas, a bucket, even a match-box (I actually saw this one day). It is all very much a frontier atmosphere, and the talk among the white settlers is frontier talk; about cattle and about the plagues of locusts that occasionally come sweeping down from Abyssinia in unbelievable clouds, about hunting, about local scandals and disasters, and about the rains.

At this great height above the equator people are said to

go a little mad at times, and there may be something in it. The sun has a clear pellucid brilliance – at 7,000 feet you can fairly see the ultra-violet rays eating into your skin – and often I felt myself being overtaken by an overpowering lassitude, an extreme desire simply to sit and dream. Then in an instant the cold damp night sets in. It ought to be soothing, the log fire, the warm eiderdown on your bed, but I found I slept restlessly. The hyrax suddenly shatters the black darkness with its terrifying cry. This animal is no bigger than a squirrel, but the noise it makes is that of a creaking door in a silent empty house. It is so jarring, so savage, so absolutely uncalled-for you can only imagine that some awful tragedy has taken place in the darkness.

And in fact the vague atmosphere of menace is always about you. This is the Mau Mau country, and it was in these highlands that the farmers during the 'emergency' used to sit at dinner with loaded and cocked revolvers on the table. It was a favourite device of the Mau Mau to slip into the room behind the servants, and so the door was kept locked from the inside. It was unlocked when the servant knocked, and he was told to wait outside until the farmer had re-sumed his seat at the table. Then with the revolver pointing steadily at his heart the servant placed the dishes on the table and the door was locked behind him when he left. One never sat before a window; one slept in the far corner of one's room, and it was also wise to change one's room every night. Three years went by like that.

The 'emergency', as it was called, is now over, yet an un-easiness persists, a feeling that a basic hostility still exists underground. I remember one night driving with friends to their farm in a remote valley in the highlands, and as we approached the house the owner said wearily, 'I wonder what has gone wrong this time while we have been away. Something always happens.' The staff, some six or seven Africans, were waiting for us with woebegone faces. 'Karmi,' they said, 'has gone.'

'Gone? Where has he gone?'

'The police came and took him.'

'But why?'

'They wouldn't say.'

This was a serious matter for my friend, since Karmi was his head-boy. For years he alone had been able to manage the milking machinery; he knew every animal on the place, every acre of ground under cultivation, and the farm could not function without him. My friend got through to the police on the telephone, and they explained the matter in a moment: 'Your head-boy turns out to be a liban.'

'But he can't be,' my friend said. 'He's been with me for years.'

'We have got evidence.'

In the end it was agreed that the boy could come back to the farm under escort and milk the cows and then return to gaol for the night.

This matter of the libans is so African, so vital a part of the whole pattern of witchcraft and ancestor worship, it is astonishing that more is not known about it. A liban is not precisely a witch doctor; he cannot enter the profession from outside. He must be born into the caste in much the same way as a Brahmin is in India, except that in Africa the caste is very small, just a handful of families. The liban is the *éminence grise* in the tribe. He cannot overrule the chief. On the other hand, it is most unlikely that the chief would ever act against his advice. Before an attack is made on another tribe, or a cattle-stealing raid, or any major decision of any kind, the liban is consulted. He dreams dreams, he consults the nebulous divine being that always lurks among the instinctive fears of the African mind, and then he pronounces his yes or no. He gives to the warriors the little bag of sacred dust which they tie to their daggers, and they then believe that they are secure from harm. If they fail on some hunt or some cattle-rustling expedition the liban is sure to point out that they have not followed his instructions correctly. If they succeed, then the liban gets the pick of the cattle and any other spoils they may have brought home.

Yet the liban is not entirely a fake. The chances are that

he really does believe that he is possessed with exceptional powers. Nearly always too he is more intelligent than the other tribesmen. He is a specialist who has been carefully trained all his life to deal with human fears and hopes, and is usually a very shrewd politician.

The importance of this man in the Mau Mau rebellion is thus quite evident. He may not have inspired the actual atrocities that were committed (and they really were as bad or even worse than anything that has happened since the African slaving days); but he did not forbid them and no one knows just how far he was committed. The British naturally rounded up the libans and their families quite early in the emergency. They were placed on a river island in Kenya and forbidden to leave it.

The explanation my friend's head-boy gave to the police was rather pathetic. He admitted that he had run away from the island some years previously. His father was dead, he said, the land there was so poor there wasn't enough to eat; and in any case he had never wanted to be a liban. And so one dark night he had made his escape and had eventually found his way to my friend's farm. He had married, and his only wish was to live a normal life like other men.

The policemen's answer to this was: once a liban always a liban; he could not escape his destiny. He might be quite innocent but his power over his companions was always there. No one would dare to disobey him, and who knew that one day he might not order them to butcher my friend and his family in their beds?

The other Africans on the farm were questioned too, and at first they denied strenuously that they knew their head-boy's real identity. But eventually they broke down and admitted yes, they knew who he was, and yes, they would have obeyed any command he chose to give them. That indeed was why the farm had been run so well.

I saw the head-boy when the police brought him back to do the milking. He was taller than the other Africans, a young man in shorts and a khaki army sweater, very thin, very black, and it was a remarkably intelligent face with high cheekbones and two narrow slits for his black eyes. His fingers were long and delicate. He stood on the lawn in front of the house and he was trembling; trembling perhaps with fear at the thought of imprisonment, or perhaps merely at the shock of his arrest and the ruin of the new life he had made for himself. The four African police in his escort were trembling too, and it was obvious that they feared that at any moment this rare and dangerous spirit by some act of magic might elude them. As for the other farm workers, they kept averting their eyes and turning their heads away. One among them perhaps – perhaps even his wife – had given the liban away to the police, and it was an awful thing.

Yet no one questioned the rightness of the police in making the arrest; the whole group seemed to accept it as an inevitable act of fate, terrible but unalterable. For a long time they stood there, hardly speaking to one another, and the liban never looked at his wife, who was carrying a child in her arms. Finally they all went off in a queer murmuring fatalistic way and disappeared at the bottom of the garden.

One wonders, of course, just how far such incidents as these are affected by the environment, not just the high altitude of these plains and their extreme remoteness from the sea, but by a kind of natural theatricality in the atmosphere. There are no ordinary seasons on the Equator – merely wets and drys – and now in March when the rains were about to break, explosive skies followed us all the way along our journey. Often there was thunder in the air, and shafts of incredibly bright sunshine shot down like spotlights through billowing curtains of heavy cloud. In the forests the flame tree and the bottle-brush tree burst out with exotic patches of scarlet, and often one saw such disparate plants as bananas and tuberoses growing side by side in the same garden. Other imported plants, bewildered by the absence of summer and winter, were simply budding and flowering as often as they could all through the year. I remember too a highly-scented shrub that put forth blossoms of three quite separate colours, white, mauve, and deep purple. It is known as the Morning, Afternoon, and Evening tree, or sometimes as the Yesterday, Today, and Tomorrow.

Then as we drove further west to Nakuru the flamingoes appeared, and this perhaps is the most colourful sight in all Africa. Tens of thousands of them were trooping about in the shallows of the lake outside the town. We saw them first from about five miles away, and they made a solid band of the palest pink on the water. Then as we drew nearer, through a forest of fever trees, the colour grew stronger and each bird was attached to its own reflection in the lake. The flamingo is a sight at once both comic and beautiful as it goes searching for its food in the mud. It stalks along very quickly with a mincing gliding motion, its long neck writhing down, its ugly lumpish head sliding along the wet surface, and it is all very reminiscent of Tenniel's drawings of the preposterous game of croquet in *Alice in Wonderland*.

If you shout and run towards the birds they take off awkwardly, pacing forward on their long legs until they have sufficient buoyancy to spread their wings. Once in the air they fly very quietly; a dense mass of them passed over our heads at twenty feet, and there was nothing to be heard but a soft rush of air like a summer breeze disturbing the leaves of a tree. Then when they want to land again they wheel into the wind, and touch down with a series of quick little trotting steps that continues for a dozen yards or so until the impulse of the flight is lost. When a thousand or more alight together in this way they make a helter skelter in the water that sounds like falling hail.

Such scenes are beautiful beyond belief, and they fill one with an intense love of Africa at times.

We reached Kisumu and were about to board the steamer that was to take us across Lake Victoria to Uganda when the rains broke at last. This was not yet the real thing – the storm lasted only half an hour and was succeeded by a fortnight of good weather – yet it seemed at the time that something had gone a little mad in nature. The lake turned black as ink, a wild wind rushed about in circles, and the sky itself joined the waves in one solid wall of water. Then in an instant it was all over, and we woke next morning far out in the lake to find that the clouds had rolled back towards the mountains. They were split at one end by a precipice of bright orange light, and along the horizon there was a layer of colour that was something between lavender and the purest apple green. Through this the sun came up. A young otter was diving for fish alongside the boat, and each time the sleek head split the surface the fur turned scarlet in the morning light.

Our chief object in Uganda was to get out to the two big game reserves which have recently been set up on the borders of the Belgian Congo. The larger of these, the Murchison Park, stretches along one of the sources of the White Nile at Lake Albert, and the other, the Queen Elizabeth, lies farther south under the peaks of Ruwenzori and the Mountains of the Moon. We hired a car in Entebbe and set out first for the Queen Elizabeth Park; and there finally we caught up with the elephants. A pair of them were grazing just outside the camp on the shores of Lake Edward when we arrived late in the afternoon, and we stopped the car about twenty yards away.

As elephants go there was, I suppose, nothing very remarkable about this couple : they were medium-sized beasts with rather short tusks, and they were feeding on a clump of bushes with that quiet aldermanic dignity that one usually associates with the species. But this hardly describes the sensations that are almost bound to overtake anyone on first seeing elephants from close at hand in their natural surroundings. One has a moment of panic, of course, but it soon passes, and presently you find yourself absorbed in the simple act of watching. Elephants, when they are not hunted or disturbed, create a curious area of calm in the bush. A kind of a hush surrounds them, an air of quiet inevitability; and this in turn seems to have a reassuring effect not only on you yourself, the observer, but upon all the other animals – the water-buck, the wildebeest, and even the warthogs – that may happen to be grazing in the same valley. It is not the dull calm of the herds of munching buffaloes. There is here a certain fastidiousness, a sense of great power used very gently and deliberately. All this no doubt can be noticed in any circus or menagerie, but nothing can quite describe the delicacy with which the wild elephant selects and breaks off the exact bunch of leaves he wants, and then stows it neatly into his tricorne mouth with a rhythmical pendulum motion of his trunk. When he has had enough of one tree and moves on to the next his footfalls never make a sound.

The other thing that surprises one during these first few minutes of elephant-watching is the nature of the country in which they live. Since the animal is so big one tends naturally to think of it against a background of vast forests and of rocks and mountains in the same relative proportions. But the trees here are scattered wide apart, and are nothing very special, and it is only at certain brief seasons of the year that the grass is as high as an elephant's eye. He stands there lording it out in the open plain for everyone to see, and his perambulation to the river for his midday bath is a progress in the grand manner, not a stealthy nervous business as it is with the other animals. From 10 a.m. until around three in the afternoon he dozes on his feet, sometimes in shade, more often in the full sunshine, gently swaying from side to side and occasionally flapping his huge ears (they are much bigger than the Indian elephant's). Towards evening he starts grazing again, and daybreak finds him feeding still. In the course of a long life of sixty or seventy years he has his full share of the miseries and grandeurs of existence – toothache and thirst, and fighting – but if left to himself he is a genuine non-aggressor. He threatens nobody and apart from being rather wasteful in the way he knocks down trees and crops causes no annoyance.

Elephants may not be as decorative as giraffe, nor as dramatic as lion, but we found that we never got tired of watching them, even when on some days they appeared in hundreds and were as commonplace as cattle. They were always easy to approach. That bright alert eye turns out to be very weak; objects barely a hundred yards away are seen only in blurred outline, and it is by his acute senses of smell and hearing that the animal becomes aware of an intruder. As you drive up to a herd every member of it will turn and face in your direction, and for a few moments, like a ballet in slow motion, there are a series of changes in the pattern of their position. The herd knows from experience that the big bulls with their valuable tusks are most likely to be shot at, and so these move into the centre. The females meanwhile take up their places on the outside, and as they do so they gather in the young calves and shoo them into the rear. As a rule the calves don't like this very much – it is hot and stuffy in the centre of the herd – and they keep straying out again through their mothers' legs. The mothers, with a casual movement of their trunks, push them back again.

It is quite easy to know when you have got too close to an elephant. The ears fan out like sails, the trunk is stretched directly and rigidly in your direction, and then, as the charge begins, it is doubled back behind the tusks. It is a fast charge – elephants can travel about fifteen miles an hour – but provided you have fifty yards start and the engine of your car does not stall you can always get away. The animal will not follow you very far.

Later on at the Tsavo Park in Kenya I got to know two young elephants fairly well. They had been picked up as babies by David Sheldrick, the game warden there, and to prevent them from being mauled by lions he stabled them at night. The male, however, made constant trouble. He bullied the smaller female, grabbing all the best food and fetching her hard slaps across the hindquarters when she attempted to protest. Sheldrick decided at length to erect a partition so that the animals could be stabled in separate stalls, but at once there was a fearful uproar. All through the night the two beasts threshed about, complaining, and it was not until Sheldrick cut a hole in the partition that they subsided. The male reached out his trunk to the female. She in turn laid her trunk on his. And so they slept.

But they still loathed being locked up at night and it was not long before the male discovered how to reach out his trunk and slide back the bolt on his door. Then he went round to the female's stall and let her out as well.

Rennie Bere, the director of the Uganda National Parks, who lives at the Queen Elizabeth Park, told me that they had had similar difficulties with elephants in his district. The animals liked to wander through the camp at night, and this was a little dangerous since often as many as thirty or forty tourists were sleeping there. A normal fence was of course useless, and so an electric wire capable of giving a smart shock was erected round the camp. The wire was attached to the general electrical system of the compound, and the current was turned off around eleven each night, but it was reckoned that once the elephants had had a shock in the earlier part of the evening they would keep away. This, however, was underrating the elephants. They soon discovered what was afoot. They waited until they saw the lights in the camp go out and then they stepped across.

At the time my wife and I reached the Queen Elizabeth camp the wire had gone, but it was not the elephants that were making a nuisance of themselves: it was the hippopotami. The lakes in the Queen Elizabeth Park contain the greatest concentration of hippopotami in existence. As soon as dusk falls thousands upon thousands of them heave their huge greyish-pink bodies out of the water, and throughout the night they graze the grass slopes along the banks. Hippopotami are not usually dangerous, not at any rate to human beings, but they can move with deceptive agility, and it is always unwise to get between them and the water.

We dined with Bere the night we arrived, and although our hut was only a couple of hundred yards from his house he would not let us walk home in the darkness. Yet the night was so still and peaceful that I could not believe at first that anything was stirring. But then Bere switched on the headlights. At once a huge form reared up before us, and as it went crashing through the huts we could see the hateful eyes of two hyenas turning away.

To see the hippopotamus best you need to take a launch along the lakes. He is a torpid beast. Most of the day he appears to do nothing very much except lie there close to the surface of the water, gently submerging and rising again, and he discloses himself from quite a long way off by a faint smell of drains. All around you as the launch proceeds you see watching eyes on the surface of the lake. They gaze moistly at you for a moment and vanish. A line of small bubbles reveals the direction the animal has taken underwater (he can stay down for as long as six minutes), and then when he emerges he makes a quick flip with his bat-like ears and a small blue geyser of water rises from his monstrous nostrils. For the most part the hippopotami live in colonies and it is nothing unusual to see groups of fifty or more wallowing on top of one another in the mud along the shallows, and a muddy hippopotamus is the muddiest thing in the world. Often they will start up a sudden conversation among themselves. The sound is a short deep monosyllabic moo with a note of protest in it, and it's quite a pleasant thing to have these grunting questions and answers following you down the river.

Bere assured me that hippopotami are not nearly as placid as they look – they fight ferociously among themselves, he said – and indeed I soon began to notice how many were scarred and torn about the backs and shoulders. Great patches of flesh were wrenched out of their hides. You notice these wounds particularly when the huge beasts rear themselves out of the water in pairs. They meet head on, their mouths wide open (the biggest mouth of any living animal), each trying to stretch his jaws wider than the other. But whether these antics were battle or love-making, or perhaps a combination of the two, it was a little difficult to say.

I asked Bere too about the fighting habits of the buffalo, but he thought they were very little to be feared. It was quite true, he admitted, that a wounded buffalo was possibly the most dangerous animal in the bush, and that they would charge a car at times, and when that great boss between the horns struck a car it was pretty well bound to go over. But in general the herds were extremely sluggish. To prove this he drove us through the midst of a couple of hundred of them one day. The thing that really reassured us about this trip was that the car was rather a grand affair which had been specially built for Queen Elizabeth and the Duke of Edinburgh when they opened the park in 1952, and Bere, we knew, did not want to get it scratched. And true enough the buffalo never moved. The old bulls indeed were rather pathetic. Their beauty, their usefulness, their virility, all was gone, and they had been cast out of the herd. They wandered about alone in a particularly dreary low-lying plain, the animal equivalent of some old-age pensioners' home, and they gazed at us with rheumy distrustful eyes. One by one, Bere explained, they were all to die, and the hyenas would eat them. They were simply waiting from day to day for the end to come.

In some ways I liked the Queen Elizabeth Park more than any other we went to. Each morning we were woken to such a fantasy of bird life that the eye grew dull at times with watching so many bright streaks of colour in the air. The smaller the birds the brighter they seemed, especially the pigmy kingfishers, the lilac-breasted rollers, the canary-yellow weaver bird, and the bee-eaters. There was one species no bigger than an ink-pot whose wings were a batik pattern of purest black and white, and always when I first opened the door of our hut at dawn a marabou stork would be standing just beyond the step, a revolting object to anyone except a besotted bird-lover, with its pendulous pouch on its scraggy neck and a look of pure bile in its eye. The white-headed fish eagle rose above us, often with a half-eaten perch in its claws, and we had only to go down to the edge of the lake to see in many hundreds such species as the Egyptian goose (that same bird that was carved in wood in Tutankhamen's tomb), the darter spreading out his wings to dry, the pelican, the ibis, the lily trotter (a bird that does just that: its long splay claws depressing the floating leaves like the keys on a piano), and the goliath heron – a misleading name to give to a creature which has the slenderness and the elegance of a Greek vase.

The Murchison Park, which lies about two hundred miles away to the north, is not so rich in bird life as this, but it has the advantage of being even more remote, and it lies in an area which has been made famous by the exploits of two of the most tenacious of African explorers, Samuel Baker and his wife. It is getting on for a hundred years since the Bakers came to this north-western corner of Uganda searching for the source of the Nile. On 4 March 1864, they sighted Lake Albert which was then an unknown inland sea, and three weeks later they discovered the Murchison Falls on the Victoria Nile. But it was another year before they could get back to civilization; for months on end one of the local chieftains held them virtually captive in the arid country which now forms the southern part of the park, and they very nearly died.

Mrs Baker had an awful time. She wore long Victorian skirts throughout, and when they became soaked in the morning dew they dragged her to the ground. Once she was unconscious with fever for a week or more, and when they were in sight of Lake Albert, the goal of their expedition, she was sucked down into a quagmire. Somehow they dragged themselves on to the shores of the lake. 'It was with extreme emotion,' Baker relates, 'that I enjoyed this glorious scene. My wife, who had followed me so devotedly, stood by my side pale and exhausted – a wreck upon the shores of the great Albert Lake that we had so long striven to reach. No European foot had ever trodden upon its sand, nor had the eyes of a white man ever scanned its vast expanse of water. We were the first; and this was the key to the great secret that even Julius Caesar yearned to unravel, but in vain. Here was the great basin of the Nile that received *every drop of water*, even from the passing shower to the roaring mountain torrent that drained from Central

Africa to the north. This was the great reservoir of the Nile!'

Then when it was all over and they were back in Egypt Baker asked himself: 'Had I really come from the Nile sources? It was no dream. A witness sat before me: a face still young, but bronzed like an Arab by years of exposure to a burning sun; haggard and worn with toil and sickness, and shaded with cares, happily now past: the devoted companion of my pilgrimage, to whom I owed success and life – my wife.'

On his return to England he was awarded the Royal Geographical Society's Gold Medal.

Except that the hostile chieftains have now been subdued, and that one can now get about in an ordinary car, nothing much has happened to change the scene in the last century. Sleeping sickness and the tsetse fly have driven away most of the inhabitants, and at the Murchison Falls, where the Victoria Nile bursts through a ravine like water breaking out of a dam, the countryside remains almost as lovely as it was when the Bakers were there in 1864. It was just below the Falls that Ernest Hemingway and his wife crashed in a small aircraft a few years ago, and they were lucky to be picked up so promptly by a passing launch.

Nowadays you come into this southern section of the park on a single track that leads northwards from the town of Masindi, and it is very wild country; on the day my wife and I arrived we were obliged to stop several times to allow herds of elephant to pass across in front of us, and Jackson's hartebeest, beautiful creatures with backward-sloping horns and a bright golden-red coat, were everywhere. The storks on their migratory flights have made this region a major staging post. They circled above us in such fantastic numbers that the sky turned dark, and when they came spiralling down for the night they covered the ground like locusts for half a mile on either side of the track. Then when we got to the bank of the Victoria Nile and sounded our car horn for the ferry to fetch us across to the camp on the opposite side we saw, for the first time in Africa, the wet snouts and eyes of the crocodiles, floating in the placid ribbon of the river.

One comes to the Murchison Park to see the crocodiles, for they are in great abundance here, and if you take a launch up to the Murchison Falls you can approach them very closely. They lie all day on the sandbanks with their mouths gaping open, and it is not until you are thirty or forty yards away that they rear up on their short legs, and with a waddling motion which has something of a clock-work toy about it, slither into the water. The water is muddy and covered with millions of little floating Nile cabbages, and so the beast entirely disappears.

I found the crocodiles so interesting that I soon got over my loathing for them; and yet with the possible exception of the hyenas they must be the meanest creatures in the African scene. They will never openly attack, and they will not even defend their own eggs; directly you attempt to land, into the water they go. It is unwise, however, to stand too close to the river bank, especially at dusk. The crocodile does not lunge out at you with his jaws; instead, having observed you carefully from midstream, he will swim sub-merged into the shallows, and with a sudden scythe-like movement of his tail he sweeps you into the water. One of the African boys in the park had been taken like this a few days before we arrived, and it was no rare thing, we were told, for baby elephants to meet their end in just this way when they came down to the river to drink. Then the mother elephant goes ranging along the bank quite power-less to retaliate.

The crocodile itself has mortal enemies, and not many of the sixty or seventy eggs which the female lays, like a turtle, in a hole in a sandbank are destined to survive. Having laid her eggs (they are rather like large white goose-eggs), the mother covers up the hole and then sometimes de-parts. This is the moment for the monitor lizard to creep out of the undergrowth, to scrape the sand away, and then to gorge himself. Even if the nest remains undiscovered the young crocodiles need a good deal of luck to survive. They come struggling to the surface of the sand, little ten-inch-long rubbery things, and make directly for the water hissing and snapping as they run. On the bank the marabou stork with his hard hangman's eye is waiting to receive them. He stands in the shallows, and with the speed of swordplay flicks them into his long bill; and if you care to watch you can descry the wriggling passage of the young crocodile down the bird's scraggy throat.

Sometimes the mother crocodile will try to defend her young at this perilous moment, and this is a fascinating thing to see. The marabou, with elaborate unconcern, stands in about six inches of water waiting for the next tit-bit to come swimming by, and from about twenty yards away the mother crocodile watches; just two murderous eyes above the surface of the stream. Then silently she submerges and comes up again about ten yards from the marabou. The bird takes no notice. And now, having carefully calculated her distance, the mother again goes down. This time she is coming in for the kill. It is a matter of about two seconds before the strike, but in those two seconds the marabou abstractedly and casually takes a backward step. At the same instant the tremendous jaws of the crocodile come rearing out of the river and snap together in the empty air at the precise spot where he was standing. Green water streaming off her back, the crocodile subsides into the river again; and the bird, with the same disingenuous air, never taking its eyes off the water at its feet, steps back to resume its meal.

Looking back now I cannot remember that I ever wanted to intervene in such incidents as these; I rather hoped that I would see a marabou get caught one day, but that was not out of any real pity for the crocodile. It was a simple desire for excitement. One develops a curious indifference, and it is always possible to dismiss the most brutal things with the phrase, 'Oh well, it's the law of nature. It's bound to happen anyway.' You lie back on the deck of the launch, the grunting hippopotami all around you, a sky of tremendous rolling thunderclouds overhead. You watch a family of elephants coming down to bathe, a line of hartebeest galloping on the skyline, a fish flopping lazily in the water; and when someone cries out, 'Look. Over there,' you follow the line of his pointing finger rather hoping that something dramatic is going on, a fight between two rutting antelopes, some act of murder.

On the ceiling of our hut there was a frightening little lizard that was coloured bright blue and vermilion, coloured so crudely that it looked as though some reckless impressionist had splashed a paint pot over the beast. It was the preoccupation of this monster to steal up on wasps and beetles and with one crunching terrifying snap swallow them alive. Often I could have warned the beetle in time. But I never did. It is the inevitability of these things, the idea that since they *do* happen it is right they should happen, that excuses you from feeling pity; and in Africa it is quite easy to let this same indifference insulate you from human tragedies as well.

These parks don't stand still: they change and evolve like any other living community. When I returned to this area a year or two later I thought that the animals were tamer than I remembered them; both crocodiles and hippopotami would allow you to approach very close before they sank beneath the surface, and the bee-eaters and the kingfishers which nest in little holes in the banks continued to fly back and forth in a whirl of scarlet and opalescent blue while our launch cruised half a dozen feet away. The behaviour of some of the elephants was strange. At the Park lodge where we dined they told us that they had been having trouble with an old male. Visitors had been feeding him with bananas, and he had developed a craving for the fruit – so much so that he used to wander through the camp towards evening in search of it. One day a guest had driven up in a Volkswagen with a branch of bananas on the back seat, and while he was in the office checking on his reservations the elephant arrived. The animal tried to open the car doors with his trunk to get at the fruit, and finding them locked picked up the vehicle and shook it angrily. Then he

threw it down. Soon after this the same elephant overturned a three-ton truck and waylaid other cars as well. It
has now been shot.

The game warden at the lodge had hardly finished telling
us his story when there was a commotion in the darkness
outside. There must have been twenty or thirty people
having dinner in the room, and now with one accord waiters
and cooks, tourists from India and Japan, western types
from Kansas, Bavaria, and France, we all hurried to the
door; and there not five yards away under the bright electric light stood a young elephant plucking at a tamarisk tree
in the car park. He was confused and agitated at so much
noise and light and movement; and the crowd of visitors,
excited by the scene, but thinking that it was a safe and
normal happening in the Park, kept drawing closer. But it
was not normal. The *must* glands on either side of the elephant's head were running, his brown eye was furious, and,
as Baker says somewhere in his books, 'the kick of an elephant is an extensive movement'. He kicked now in the
empty air, and the crowd drew back a little with just such
a gasp as you heard sometimes in a circus when the lion
snarls and springs, or the man on the flying trapeze
launches himself on a triple somersault. But there seems to
be a kind of bright mesmerism about danger at these
moments, and we all moved towards the elephant again.
He lifted up his trunk then and shrieked. It was so outlandish a noise, so savage and spontaneous that I think we
would all have turned then and bolted had not the animal
himself wheeled round, and in a moment his grey shape had
dissolved into the darkness beyond the electric light.

Later again that night I saw him moving very softly
among the huts where the visitors sleep. He overturned a
rubbish bin by the kitchen door, and then stood swaying as
though he was contemplating some other, more defiant
move. All this was a great joke in the camp – an elephant
rooting about like a stray dog for scraps – and yet it could
be that there was something unresolved here, a very African
thing; the too sudden conjunction of civilization with

savagery. On the surface it looks all right, the wild animal among the rubbish bins, the tribesman in a city suit, and familiarity breeds, if not contempt, a specious atmosphere of safety. But then in an instant and without warning, the link snaps, the façade of understanding proves too flimsy, and the animal strikes, the Mau Mau warrior runs amok, and it is not a joke; co-existence becomes mutual murder.

For my own part I prefer the animals well away from the civilized scene in Africa, and the half-domesticated elephant gives me less pleasure to recall than the white rhinoceros which we saw in the wilds outside the Park. This was close to a place called Pakwach – the Leopard's Place – to which we now proceeded in yet another river steamer, the *Lugard*. All the western bank of the river from Lake Albert to the Sudan border at Nimule, a distance of about 180 miles, has been a great place for white rhinoceroses in the past, but it is getting a little difficult to find them now; they are a mighty source of meat for the local tribes. We searched all day with the local game warden, travelling over ground that defeated our four-wheel driven vehicles at times, before we came on a single lonely specimen. But he was terrific. He stood in a field of black cotton soil above the river and he was accompanied by a snow-white ibis which paced behind him when he walked and jumped on to his back when he chose to run. Probably he had never seen a car before and he was very wild. He made a little run towards us and then veered off, snorting. He would have bolted then, had we got out of the car and enabled him to catch the human smell; but as things were he was confounded and a little enraged by the strange shapes and noises of the vehicles. He kept on bolting towards us, wheeling away suddenly and then facing forward again. A storm burst on us while we were watching him – one of those African storms which are so insanely violent you feel that something has gone mad in nature – and we were a little worried as we slithered about in the black mud that he might come on again at us and this time go through with his charge. But instead he decided to move away. He trotted off with all the power and majesty of a great loco-motive on the move, or better still a battleship in a rough sea, and the hail rattled off his hide as though it had hit solid steel. The good thing about this splendid sight was that it was a natural and primitive display of a great beast in his own element; and it is no wonder now that a last-minute effort is being made to keep at least a few specimens alive, for they survive practically nowhere else in Africa and already their numbers are down to two or three hundred. The plan is to catch a batch of them with snares and ropes and then transport them into Murchison Park, where they should be safe from poachers and hunters. The problem here is that no one quite knows how the *black* rhinoceroses, who live in the Park, will behave. They may resent the intrusion of the white species and fight. Personally, I am never able to tell the difference between a black and a white rhinoceros, to me they are both plain battleship grey, but it is commonly said that the black variety is the more aggressive of the two. Be this as it may, the obvious solution of the rhinoceros problem is to establish the two species on different sides of the Nile within the Park, for they are not willing swimmers; and this no doubt is the experiment which will soon be made.

But it was not only the animals in the Park that were changed — or being changed; the visitors too had altered. On my first visit it was a relatively simple and primitive place, but the second time it was crowded with tourists, mostly Hindus, who had driven up from Kampala and the other towns in Southern Uganda. Most of them do not come to see the animals. It is the Nile itself that attracts them, possibly because some of Gandhi's ashes were thrown into the river below Lake Victoria some years ago; these people engage launches in the Park and travel upstream for a few miles until they reach the point where the river rushes through a chasm barely twenty feet across, and flings great clouds of spray into the air. These falls, the Murchison Falls, have an extreme fascination for the Hindus, for they sit and gaze at them as though held by a spell. Then they return to their cars and drive home again. It is very curious, a re-creation of the holy Ganges in the midst of pagan Africa.

From the Murchison Park we went on to the little town-ship of Arua which lies in an enclave of Uganda that is wedged in between the Belgian Congo and the Sudan. But here at least one can see that rarest of all sights in Africa – the local people living more or less in a state of nature. It is very far from being primitive. Here as everywhere the Indian traders have arrived, and most of the African men wear the horrible uniform that has been bestowed on them by civilization : a tattered cotton shirt and a pair of derelict shorts. But in the fields and in the smaller villages many of the women still wear only a couple of clumps of leaves – one clump aft and the other before – attached to a thong around their waists. It is a costume that is gathered freshly from the trees each day, and it is quite astonishingly gay and chic. Nearly always the young girls carry water gourds or brightly coloured packages on their heads as they walk about the plantations. Their greeting is a wide-open toothy smile, and to my vagrant mind the scene was like nothing so much as some of the lusher spectacles in the Folies Bergère in Paris.

There seem to be no definite rules about this matter of clothing. East of Arua, towards the frontier of Abyssinia, we found later other tribes where no woman will go naked but the men wear nothing below the waist at all. Then again, just a few miles away to the west is the Belgian Congo, the fashion alters once more : both men and women have a passion for beaded ornaments and flowing robes of the most hectic hue. On every woman's back – and the word every is hardly an exaggeration – a baby is riding in a sling of cotton cloth. Even now I find it difficult to think of the Congo without conjuring up a vision of innumerable little black cannon-ball heads pressed into the women's shoulders.

You begin to notice many other changes soon after you cross the border from British territory into the Congo. In the main, Uganda is rather a serious place, and the prevailing colour of the landscape, especially during the long dry seasons, is a dusty brown. Here perhaps more than anywhere Christian missionaries have worked with a special fervour, and there is a vaguely institutional air about many of the villages and settlements.

The Congo, on the other hand, is green with a frantic greenness, and one's first impression on arriving there is of a certain lightening of the atmosphere, a sense of plenty and well-being. And this is queer, because the Belgians have imposed a discipline, almost a subservience, on the Africans which goes far beyond anything the British have attempted. The men stop and salute or raise hats whenever a white traveller goes by, a thing that rarely happens in Kenya or Uganda. In the Belgian game parks and the hotels the African staff is paraded like a squad of soldiers with the blast of a bugle or a whistle at first light in the morning. Then, too, the main road that leads you in from Uganda to the Ruwenzori area is a highly conventional road, a boulevard dotted with familiar road signs, and except for the elephant grass and the occasional mud huts on either side you might easily imagine that you were back in Europe. All is neat and well cared for, the grass is cut, the palm trees neatly spaced, the plantations arranged in well-ordered rows.

The actual border, however, is rather a deserted place. No Africans are allowed to live there, because all this region is embraced by the great Albert Game Park, and the Belgian customs guard leads a solitary life. He was eager for conversation on the day we arrived. 'You see that slope up there?' he said. 'Fifty elephant passed that way this morning.' And again, 'We had a leopard here last week.' And still again, 'Would you like to come and see my garden?' It was a wonderful garden. It bloomed with custard apples, hibiscus, wild tulips, and bananas, and the incredibly sweet scent of Persian lilac hung in the air. There was a big native drum on the veranda, its skin of waterbuck hide worn bare with beating, and all around us tumultuous mountains spread away. But it was not enough to beguile loneliness, to keep the cafard at bay.

As he handed my passport back, the customs man said, 'I see you were born in Australia. That must be a wonderful country.'

'Parts of it,' I said, 'are quite like Africa in many ways.'

He looked at me in dismay.

This is a recurring theme all through this part of the continent: this besetting loneliness in the midst of plenty. Most of the officials in the game reserves are devoted men; they have taken on their jobs chiefly because they are absorbed in wild life, and perhaps too because they are captivated by Africa itself. For days, even weeks on end, they are out in the bush and they see no one but their own African assistants and occasional tribesmen. Even their homes in the parks are isolated places, especially during the wet season when no visitors arrive. The house generally is a modern brick affair, a single-storey bungalow such as you might see in any newly developed garden suburb; and it is quite startling to find so many familiar things in the midst of this wilderness: the bright chintz curtains on the windows, the bookcase, the cushions and armchairs, the plastic screen around the shower, the pile of magazines of the Good-Housekeeping Homes-and-Gardens variety. Everything suggests the woman's touch. But then quite often there is no woman. It is not tactful to inquire about this because there usually lurks in the background a familiar and painful story. Sure enough the young wife was here; she came out from Europe and for the first year or two probably she loved the place. She was engrossed in getting the house in order and in the advantages of being an official's wife in Africa – the car they could never have afforded at home, the extra money to spend, the domestic servants. At first too there may even have been a certain attraction in having elephants and herds of antelope for neighbours instead of Mrs Smith and Mrs Robinson. But presently she missed the shops, the cinema down the road, the pleasure of talking to another woman, not necessarily a dozen other women, just one would have been enough. But now there is no point in wearing a new dress, and there are no guests to invite to the large new dining-table; none but the other men in the park whose store of casual dinner-table conversation has been exhausted long ago. And so eventually, out of hopeless boredom, a half-guilty hysteria of loneliness, she has gone away. The husband remains. He remains not too happily nor very easily but still he has his job.

In many ways the Belgians in the Congo have made rather a better effort in meeting this problem than the British. Where Africa has pressed too heavily upon them they have resolutely shut it out, or rather they have taken hold of Africa and forced it to their own designs. With the Latin talent for family life they have bothered tremendously about their homes, planting flowers and vegetable gardens, keeping up a high standard of food and imported wine, living in fact as closely as they can to the life they left behind them in Belgium. In a certain sense they give the impression that they are embarked on a military expedition of some kind. There is a great come and go of officials. District commissioners arrive in a flurry of uniforms and salutes; and at the parades and official banquets Madame la Colonelle will appear in a smart little ensemble which would have been equal to a day's racing at Longchamps or a week-end house-party in the Ardennes.

We stayed at one quite staggering hotel just across the border and at the foot of the Ruwenzori range. A mountain torrent spanned by rustic bridges rushed through the garden. From the swimming-pool and the tennis-court where waiters with drinks were padding about one could look straight up through driving mists to the perpetual snow on the heights of Ruwenzori, some twelve thousand feet above. There was a bar of the French bistro type on the veranda, and the food was excellent.

I remember all this luxury with particular clarity because on the next day we went to see the pygmies, and to my mind the pygmies are just about the most primitive sight in Africa. There was no difficulty in finding them. We simply drove a few miles down the road to a place called Beni, and at the sound of our car horn they came running out of the forest – dozens of them, men, women, and toy-sized children. They were quite naked, and, being used to tourists, immediately crowded round the car and asked for money.

There is, I suppose, a certain fascination about the *idea* of pygmies, but nobody in Africa had warned me of what it was like to meet them face to face. They smell like no other living creatures on earth, and it is not the sort of smell that can be politely ignored. Then, too, it is not so much their smallness that impresses you : it is their shape and by no indulgence can this be called anything but repulsive. With their swollen stomachs, their spindly little legs, and their clutching hands, they remind you somewhat of the gnomes and gargoyles on medieval cathedrals in Europe. To be fair, one has to admit that the pygmies are friendly and cheerful people, and that they have the reputation of being great hunters; they move like shadows through the jungle. But I don't think I am curious about pygmies any more. If you have seen one you have seen them all.

We headed south after this, and a long day's drive brought us to Lake Kivu. Kivu is a lovely pool of green water, and it is set among some of the most splendid forests and mountains of all Africa. From time to time one of the many volcanoes nearby will erupt, and you can see the places where the lava streams, having burnt up everything in their path, have gone hissing and steaming into the lake. Tropical flowers bloom here with a special luxuriance, and the market-places of the villages are blazing with highly coloured fruit. But these are not the things that particularly strike your eye as you arrive at one of the lakeside towns, at Kisenyi for example. At Kisenyi you behold the astonishing metamorphosis of Africa into Europe. It has been brilliantly done. A boulevard with flowering gardens has been built around the lake with the line of hotels and villas on one side and on the other the *plage*. On the *plage* a number of coloured parasols are dotted about, and out on the lake itself people are diving from rafts and sailing about in motor-boats. Close to the club on the beach there is a miniature golf-course, and the low moan of rock 'n' roll comes softly through the trees.

Lake Kivu, of course, is only a tiny dot in this immense landscape, and the rest of the Congo, a country one-third the size of the United States, is for the most part extremely wild and savage country. Yet the place does give one a startling glimpse of the headlong pace at which things are happening in Africa now. Eighty years ago no white man had even seen this lake, the slave trade was still flourishing, and the local chieftains might have been residing on the moon for all they knew about the outside world. Within living memory Stanley, probably the greatest of all African explorers, very nearly died of starvation and exposure in these forests, and as late as the nineteen-twenties Carl Akeley, the American naturalist, led his last expedition here in search of the mountain gorilla. Akeley lies buried among the extinct volcanoes above the lake. All this sounds like the wildest fantasy now.

The change has been so sudden and so devastating that it has left the Africans a little dazed. They are of course a dominating part of this scene, and yet in an odd way they are not exactly of it any more. Somewhere along the way they seem to have become lost between the two worlds of the ritual dance and the water-ski-ing tourists on the lake, and where the Belgians have encouraged them to cling to their ancient habits a weird kind of surrealism sets in.

You notice this particularly among the Watusi tribe at Lake Kivu. The Watusi are celebrated hunters, very tall and lithe and energetic, and for a sum which is roughly equivalent to £25 they can be induced to perform their war dance. A party of about twenty of us went out to see them one day, and it was an odd experience. The performance was given in the open among a grove of young trees that looked absurdly like the Bois de Boulogne in Paris in the spring, and we sat on wooden benches with our cameras in hand. Presently the warriors arrived in their war paint, with a drummer at their head, and for the next half hour they waved their assagais and in formation thumped their hard feet on the ground. It was wonderful timing, and the rhythmic movement of their feathered headdresses was a remarkable thing to see. And yet it was not real. It had neither the vicarious reality of the theatre nor any reality in life. There had been no war to justify this war dance, nothing to inspire them except their professional skill and perhaps the thought of the £25; and so they were a little self-conscious in the way that children sometimes are when, against their instincts, they have been persuaded to dress up and make a performance at a party. After a while the dancers drifted away rather lamely through the trees.

On the way back to town we passed another group of Watusi who had been playing football that afternoon. They were wearing white shorts and striped sweaters and they looked, I thought, a good deal more natural and cheerful than their befeathered and painted fellow-tribesmen in the woods. Without much reluctance we went back to Nairobi in the morning.

CHAPTER THREE

A PLEISTOCENE DAY

NAIROBI is the safari capital of Africa. This is the base where most of the hunters, the photographers, and the ordinary run-of-the-mill sightseers assemble their vehicles and their equipment before they set off into the blue. You can travel very simply if you like, driving your own car and stopping for the night at country inns along the way. Camping, on the other hand, is more complicated and expensive and involves problems over petrol, water, and food. Quite a number of people, however, get about with caravans or hunting cars that are fitted with beds, tents, and cooking gear, and usually they take a couple of African boys along with them. Finally, you can go to one of the safari companies and travel *au grand luxe* complete with a white hunter and a regular entourage of servants. The East Africa Tourist Travel Association recently put out a booklet about these trips, and it contains some revealing passages.

'He (the hunter),' it says, 'can have radios, refrigerators, electric light, air mattresses, and every comfort. Well-cooked five-course meals are served attractively; hunting clothes are laundered each day and soft-footed servants wait on his every need . . .

'In general, it may be said that with every luxury possible, a safari for one person costs approximately £27 a day inclusive, except for alcohol and tobacco. As very little extra equipment is needed to handle two persons, the price drops to about £21 a day each.

'The normal routine of camp life is to rise about 5.30 a.m., breakfast on fruit, cereal, bacon and eggs, and coffee at 6, and leave camp when dawn is breaking about 6.30 a.m.; this period of the morning is fresh and crisp, the animals are grazing freely in the open, and the light is still soft.

'After 10 or 11 a.m. the game disappears for a rest, and the sun is too warm for exercise to be pleasant, so, unless following an elephant or tracking some elusive and rare species, the hunters themselves usually return to camp for a rest and lunch. After which they again go out to be ready to greet their quarry about 4 p.m., at which time the game wakes up and grazes towards the waterholes.'

Women are advised to stick to neutral colours in their clothes or they will agitate the game. If you don't happen to have a rifle you can rent one for around £15 a month; on top of that there is the hunting licence. A full game licence in Kenya in recent years cost £50 and entitled you to 3 bushbeck, 3 duiker, 1 Grant's gazelle, 1 gerenuk, 2 Coke's hartebeest, 3 impala, 1 klipspringer, 1 oribi, 1 beisa oryx, 2 pigmy antelope, 2 common reedbuck, 1 serval cat, 1 steinbuck, 2 topi, 6 Thomson's gazelle, 1 defassa waterbuck, 2 wildebeest, and 4 common zebra.

Additional licences must be obtained if you want to go after elephant (£75 for the first one, £100 for the second), rhinoceros (£40 each), leopard (£40), hippopotamus (£10), buffalo (5s.), lion (£25), ostrich (£2-10), the blue monkey (£1).*

Since the war lion and leopard have become increasingly rare, and it is practically unheard of for a man to shoot out his full licence (which he has to pay for anyway whether he kills the animals or not); still, he is pretty well certain of bagging a dozen or more specimens of different species, and in the course of a month he will cover about 1,500 miles and see a number of remarkable things. Even if you prefer to photograph rather than hunt (and an increasing number of people do nowadays), it can be just as exciting; you have to get rather nearer the game. A safari, in fact, is probably the most rewarding adventure you can buy anywhere, and although a three months' trip for four clients and two white hunters may cost as much as £6,500 (including a fairly stiff tip to the staff at the end), there is no shortage

* The game laws alter from year to year; the prices quoted may have risen since the above was written.

of customers. Some of the larger safari firms in Nairobi are booked a year in advance. Americans are the chief clients.

In normal circumstances I do not think that my wife and I, on our journey through Africa, would have dreamed of going on a full-dress safari of this kind; we usually travelled by train or by ourselves in hired cars, and in any case we were not interested in shooting. In Nairobi, however, one of the best-known white hunters, Donald Ker, invited us to go out with him on a month's trip as his guests. Ker, a small compact man now in his early fifties, is an interesting case. Having spent half a lifetime hunting in the bush – at the age of sixteen he was already out on his own, sometimes for months at a time, shooting elephant – he cannot now bear to destroy a wild animal of any description, except for food; and even that he does with reluctance. His chief interest now is the study of wild life in its natural surroundings, and with this end in view he proposed a fascinating trip to the extreme south-western corner of Kenya. Here is an area of some six thousand square miles which for a long time has been a kind of island in the centre of the continent.

This is some of the finest land in all Africa, a network of forested rivers and great open plains that slope gently down to Lake Victoria, but there are no roads and because of the tsetse fly no one has ever lived there. Wild animals are not affected by the fly, and so they have been left to roam the country pretty well undisturbed for occasional hunting parties coming down from Nairobi in the dry season, and gangs of African poachers who operate along the shores of the lake.

When the Mau Mau emergency began in 1952 this region became doubly remote; some of the Kikuyu tribesmen were in hiding there, and orders were issued by the British authorities forbidding anyone to go near the place. By the time we got there, however, things had quietened down considerably, and Ker had been given permission to visit the forbidden area. A few of the Mau Mau were still hanging about in the forest, Ker said, but they were known to be without ammunition, and in any case the authorities had arranged for a couple of native police to go along with him in addition to his own boys. He proposed to wander about through this virgin territory for two or three weeks before moving northward towards the Abyssinian border.

By early January the safari was assembled in Nairobi and everything was ready. It was not, Ker explained regretfully, like a safari in the old days. Then, everyone in town turned out to see you off. No cars of course; the client riding on a mule and a hundred boys with bundles on their heads strung out down the main road in front of the town's one hotel. A squad of soldiers or askaris went first, and a sort of jester with a musical horn moved up and down the line to lead the singing and keep the porters happy. Every twenty miles or so they dropped off a group of men to form a camp, and in the end these camps might be stretched across several hundred miles of country. Like ants the porters kept up a constant come and go along the route, some of them bringing back trophies from the shooting party in the wilds, others coming up from Nairobi with supplies. Sometimes sportsmen would stay out in the field for six months or more and never see another white man. That was the way President Theodore Roosevelt, one of the greatest of hunters, had done it when he came out to collect specimens for the Smithsonian Institute in 1909.

Ker's outfit was not so impressive as this, and no one came to see us off; still, we were probably better equipped than the Roosevelt party. Ker and my wife and I rode in front in a hunting car with Saidi, his head-boy, and a five-ton lorry followed on behind. The lorry was loaded with sleeping and dining tents, food and fuel supplies for a month, a good deal of heavy equipment for making repairs and getting across rivers and swamps, and of course a medicine chest. Such of the ten boys who could not get into the cabin of the lorry were perched on top of the baggage. The sun was shining and morale was high.

It was Ker's idea to take a roundabout route to our objective, travelling southwards first to the Tanganyika border and then moving westward across the Serengeti Plains towards Lake Victoria. We were to stop just short of the lake at a place called Ikoma, on the Grumeti River, and then strike northwards into the unmapped and uninhabited country. All this first part of the journey has been pretty well known to travellers for the past thirty years, and the roads and the well-worn tracks give you a sense of familiarity and security. It is a vast space, but space that has been tamed and civilized. Yet it is impossible to travel far in this part of Africa without something outlandish happening. On our first night, for instance, when we were camping under Kilimanjaro, I was introduced to a special breed of leather-eating hyenas. Hyenas, heaven knows, are capable of anything, and their own flesh is said to be so repulsive that even vultures will reject it if they can get anything else. Hyenas prey upon the young, the weak, and the dying, and no carcass is too rotten for their taste. Here around this camp there was no shortage of food; we had seen a dozen different varieties of antelope moving around the waterholes just as the daylight was fading, and the baboons were in hundreds. Yet this particular breed of hyenas around our camp was said to have a special predilection for good solid tanned boot leather. I did not altogether believe this, but when I went to my tent that night I tucked my own shoes (a thick-soled pair bought just a month before in London) well under my camp-bed.

Sleeping under canvas in the African bush is a special experience until you get used to it. The leopard coughs in the darkness. The hyenas grunt and snarl and whoop as they prowl about. A faint flicker of rose light from the camp-fire strikes the canvas above your head, and you hear, or think you hear, the first distant throaty roar of a hunting lion – though of this you cannot be quite sure because the noise is very similar to the deep voices of the African boys who sit on, hour after hour, around the fire telling endless stories to one another, and pausing only, when the leopard comes near, to throw another log on the flames. One thing at least is tolerably certain : wild animals loathe and fear the human smell, and although they may approach quite close out of sheer curiosity they will not come into the camp itself. Often in the morning you will see the tracks of some large animal, a rhinoceros perhaps, not fifty yards from your tent. The tracks, a series of large rosettes in the dust, come on very steadily until suddenly the animal has picked up the hateful scent in the air, and you can see where he has wheeled sharply away into the bush.

It seemed therefore incomprehensible to me on this night that I should have been woken by a strange presence in the tent. It was not so much a presence as a smell; a smell so vile, so absolutely sickening, it appeared for an instant to be an imaginary thing, part of a particularly bad dream perhaps. I groped for a flashlight and something an inch or two away from my face vanished into the darkness. All this was a great joke in the morning when the boys searched everywhere and found not so much as a trace of a hobnail from my shoes. Even the rubber heels had been eaten. After that I slept with my second pair of shoes inside my bed.

Hyenas have amazing savagery and determination. One alone will drive away a cheetah, the great spotted cat which is the fastest thing alive. (When some years ago cheetahs were raced against greyhounds in England the cheetahs jumped clean over the greyhounds' backs to get to the front.) Two hyenas will force a leopard to abandon a kill; a dozen of them will defeat a lion. Once Ker and I in our car headed off a hyena that was about to pounce on a baby Thomson's gazelle, and we chased it for upwards of six miles at twenty miles an hour, round and round in circles on open ground. It was not even breathing hard when we stopped at last. And when it turned its dark muzzle over its shoulder towards us, looking at us without rage or fear, simply accepting, as wild animals do, the instant prospect of death, we were a little ashamed.

Part of Ker's aversion to shooting is tied up with this matter of pursuing animals in cars. In earlier times – and not so far back as Roosevelt either – you tracked your quarry sometimes for scores of miles and for days or weeks on end. In a certain sense you earned the trophy. Now you drive along in comfort until you find your buffalo or your rhinoceros and the law requires you to walk only five hundred yards away from your car before you shoot. Very little exertion and not much danger is involved. Neither hunger nor any great skill in tracking brings you to the kill; and somewhere in all this the true excitement dies away.

I began to see Ker's point quite unexpectedly a day or two after we had left Kilimanjaro behind us and were moving west through cultivated country on the edge of the Great Rift Valley. We were six thousand feet up and a cold rain was falling. Across the muddy soil a stray gazelle buck came running, and a young African tribesman, naked except for a cloth around his waist, started up in pursuit. Normally the man would never have had a ghost of a chance of catching the buck, but perhaps he thought the mud would slow it up and anyway this meant a month's supply of meat. Man and animal went flying across the skyline at tremendous speed, bounding from one tussock to another, and they must have gone half a mile or more when the buck took an unlucky turn towards a group of native huts. A woman came out with a spear in her hand, and as he rushed past the young man grabbed it out of her hand like a runner in a relay race. He disappeared finally, his spear held high and a barking dog at his heels, over the curve of the hill. The buck was still going well and I don't think the young man ever caught up. Yet he was a real hunter, almost a figure from a classical frieze with that straining back, and one wished him luck, one would have liked to have seen him launch the spear and the kill would have been a good kill at the peak of a concentrated excitement.

All this country – the Great Rift Valley around the Ngoro-ngoro crater mountain and the Serengeti plains that stretch away to the west – has been the scene of immemorial hunting, possibly the earliest hunting anywhere on earth. A German scientist, a man with the engaging name of Professor Kattwinkel, appears to have been the first to have discovered this. He walked up from Dar-es-Salaam on the coast somewhere about 1911, and having made his way out on to the Serengeti Plains, came on the deep water-course which is now known as the Olduvai Gorge. Looking up from the dry bed of the river to the three-hundred-foot cliffs on either side the Professor found himself confronted with fossils of immense antiquity. There were the remains of the *deinotherium*, a huge elephant with tusks in the lower jaw pointing downwards like a walrus, the *metaschizotherium*, a creature with five-toed feet related to the rhinoceros, the *savatherium*, a giraffe with a short neck and antlers that branched out to a distance of six feet, the *bularchus*, a giant ox, and the *pelorovis*, a sheep the size of a modern buffalo with a twelve-foot spread of horns. All these beasts, which have long since become extinct, had been hunted by stone-age men. (Their sharpened stones and stone axeheads can still be picked up in the gorge by the dozen.)

Kattwinkel's discovery caused something of a sensation when he returned to his home in Munich, and with the backing of the Kaiser a German called Dr Hans Beck organized an expedition to Olduvai. Beck's work was cut short for a time by the First World War, when British and German forces were engaged in battles close to Olduvai for the possession of Tanganyika, but in the early thirties Dr L. S. B. Leakey, the Curator of the Corydon Museum in Nairobi, returned to the site, and he has been making excavations there ever since. Leakey, a scientist of world repute, has made some startling discoveries, and he firmly believes that here or hereabouts will eventually be found the very earliest traces of mankind. Quite apart from the prehistoric animals there is evidence that human habitation in the region goes back at least 250,000 years. These early men hunted in packs like wolves. It was their practice to drive the animals into defiles and swamps, where they became bogged in the mud and easily killed. Later the *bolas* was invented, a weapon that is still used by the Eskimos and the Patagonians. It consists of three or more rounded pebbles, which are attached together by thongs. These were flung at the quarry, and when its legs became entangled it was brought to the ground. Then it was a simple matter with a sharp stone to skin and quarter the carcass, which was eaten raw. (When this theory was challenged on the ground that the animals were too fleet for a man to catch, and their hides too tough to be cut with a stone, Leakey, a former footballer, responded by giving a personal demonstration; he chased a Grant's gazelle on foot one day, and after a short run brought it down with a flying tackle. He then skinned the animal with a stone in a matter of fifteen minutes.)

Later again the hunters began to depict their exploits in drawings and paintings on the surfaces of overhanging rocks where they would be secure from the weather. In Tanganyika there are dozens of these decorated rock-shelters which have not been fully explored yet. They contain drawings which are not unlike those in the caves at Lascaux in France – the same free outline and spirited movement, the same warm colours made from such mixtures as red ochre and grease. Many of these sketches are very gay and charming. Hunting is the persistent theme, and it seems possible that there was a certain superstition here; if a wounded animal got away in the darkness the hunter might well have wished to fix its image in a drawing, believing that thus it would stop its flight, and that its tracks would be easily picked up again in daylight on the following morning. The practice of sticking pins into the wooden or clay images of one's enemies appears to have come later.

The special charm of Olduvai is that nothing very much has happened there in the last few hundred thousand years, at any rate as far as man is concerned. As the Ice Age receded the ground thawed out, the sivatherium and the other monsters died, but the lion, leopard, hyena, wild dog, and serval cat lived on (and incidentally they have not changed much in size or shape since prehistoric times). In Northern Africa the ancient Egyptian civilization came and went, but nothing was recorded here, and right up to the start of this century the local tribes had made very little advance beyond the stone-age. For some reason, perhaps the lack of water and sparseness of the population, the Arab slave routes did not pass through the Serengeti, and the early explorers like Burton and Thompson tended to keep either to the south or the north of Olduvai Gorge. Theodore Roosevelt, who turned up in East Africa a good twelve months ahead of Professor Kattwinkel, was much struck with this enduring primitiveness. At the end of one of his early marches into the wilds he exclaims in his diary, 'A Pleistocene day!'

Leakey's view is that the drying up of the Sahara has had much to do with the isolation of Africa and the consequent backwardness of animal and native life there. Once the Sahara swarmed with all kinds of wild game, and the lions which were captured by the Romans (Pompey once paraded no less than 600 of them in the Colosseum), surely came from northern Africa as well as the Middle East. The Roman elephants too were African elephants, and it is something of a wonder that they could have been trained in battle, or that Hannibal could have induced them to cross the Alps, since today it is the hardest thing in the world to tame the African elephant, and very few people ever attempt it.

All this region around the Olduvai Gorge is wonderfully unspoiled country, mostly scrub and open grassland, and except for a few mud huts of the Masai tribe it is uninhabited. It is the essence of Africa. At midday the flat-topped acacia trees stand in absolute stillness on the empty land, and the horizon becomes lost in a floating mirage. Then, in the softer light of the evening, the distant hills take shape, and a blue haze gathers on every rock and cliff that juts above the plain.

It is said that in every country there is one particular

thing which is so commonplace that no one speaks about it, and for me in Africa it is this blue haze. It haunts the early morning and the evening, and it gives one an intense feeling of liberation, of immense uncharted distances through which one would like to go on moving indefinitely, and without object, simply letting the time go by.

But the really spectacular thing at this eastern end of the Serengeti Plains is the Ngorongora Crater mountain. Its circular rim rises 8,000 feet above the sea, and on the day we arrived heavy rain clouds were hanging about. Presently, however, the sun broke through, and from the top of the rim we were able to look down over the other side on to the bright green floor of the crater, 2,000 feet below. At first sight this crater floor does not seem to be very big – it is not unlike an ordinary circular football field seen from a seat high up in the grandstand – and it is difficult to believe that the actual area is 200 square miles. Nothing appears to move down there; it is as calm and silent as a mountain lake.

Ker decided to camp on the top for the night, and then go down into the crater on the following day. We could not make a direct descent – there was a gang of African convicts working on a motor-road but it was not finished yet – and so we had to make a twenty-mile journey round the rim of the crater to a point on the opposite side where there was a rough track leading downwards. With chains fixed to the wheels of the vehicles we set off in the first light of the morning. The convicts, I noticed, were already at work.

'No trouble about keeping them in at night,' Ker said; 'with so many elephant and rhinoceros about they don't even have to guard them.'

Yet there was no elephant or rhinoceros. Their tracks were clear enough on the sodden ground, but the forest was very thick and we saw nothing much except an occasional francolin, which is a queer little bird that runs with a rolling nautical gait like a man with his hands in his trouser pockets. There was no sound or sign of movement anywhere. A couple of hours went by like this and it was all rather disappointing.

But now we turned down along a steep and rocky track, and a few minutes later our car suddenly emerged from the trees into the bright sunshine on the floor of the crater. And there, spreading out before us, was a stupendous field of grass on which, at a guess, some ten thousand wild animals were roaming.

Nothing in Africa quite prepares you for this apparition. It is as though a curtain has been suddenly lifted on a brightly-lit stage; the eye falters for a moment and you must look again, a second and a third time, before you begin to comprehend what is happening. The wild animals don't take much notice of the vehicles. It may be as you drive quietly over the grass you may start the wildebeest off on one of their many gallops, that the baboons will bark at you and the elephants will fan out their ears suspiciously at the sound of the car. But here you are no more than one in a multitude, and you are as secure as Noah in his ark. The animals are engrossed in their own lives, and if the hyena, with his curious sloping walk, gives you a look of hate that is because he probably hates all living things. Even here the hyenas have a skulking air that suggests the whole world is against them – which it probably is.

Ker stopped the car on a patch of rising ground for a while, and we just sat there, looking. The sun was still shining. I fancy that, like a good and successful showman, Ker was just as pleased with my astonishment as I was myself. With a matter-of-fact air he let in the clutch and drove off across the plain, saying that we ought to come across a lion or two; there were about thirty in the crater.

It was the first lion that we met that I particularly remember. He was a huge, black-maned beast, and he was stretched out comfortably on the grass on his four paws like a monumental statue. Evidently he had just eaten, for when we approached to within twenty yards he did nothing more than favour us with a slow and casual stare. Then the yellow eyes closed, the jaws opened in a wide yawn, and in a deep daze of weariness the animal rolled over on his back. All around him in the sunshine herds of zebras and gazelles were quietly grazing. The hyenas sat and waited.

It was a little later in the morning that we saw the other side of this picture. We were driving along a watercourse on the opposite side of the crater when another lion got up suddenly in front of us, a younger beast with very little mane as yet, but he looked very fine as he lifted his head and made the air vibrate with a deep short throaty roar. Ker stopped the car at once. 'Now watch,' he said, 'he's hunting.' Over to the left, some two hundred yards away from the lion, a mingled herd of zebra and wildebeest were grazing, and they were now standing very still with their heads turned towards the point of danger. But for the moment the lion did nothing more. He sank down on his haunches and gently sniffed the breeze. Then again he got up in full view of his quarry, moved forward with a few slow paces, and again emitted his awful threatening growl. This time the zebras and the wildebeest bolted. They ran full tilt for fifty yards or so and then turned uncertainly and faced the lion again. Ker explained what was happening.

'You feel the breeze? It's blowing directly over the herd towards that gully over there; and in that gully somewhere a lioness is waiting. She is the one that will make the kill. She will wait until her mate has driven the zebras on to her hiding place and then she'll spring out on the nearest animal.'

'But don't the zebras know what is happening? Don't they ever learn from experience?'

'No, they never learn.'

It was obviously going to be a long business – perhaps a couple of hours or more – and we did not wait for the kill. In any case Ker explained that our chances of seeing the lioness spring were not very good. Up to the last minute one never knew exactly where to look, and it would all be over in an instant; just that one quick bound on to the victim's back and that terrible cat-claw reaching down to the zebra's eyes and mouth. Then probably the lion would come loping across the plain to join his mate and settle, roaring, on to the dying beast.

We missed all this, but we saw the aftermath when we came back in the afternoon, and that was fascinating. The victim – it turned out to be a wildebeest and not a zebra – had not long been dead, and two lions were squatting side by side on their haunches and tearing at the meat. All around us, in the sky as well as on the ground, the im- memorial pattern of a kill was forming. There was a ring of jackals round the carcass, and from time to time one of them would dart in and seize a titbit from under the lions' jaws. The lions did not seem to mind this particularly; just once the female rose abruptly and made a tremendous swipe at one of the jackals that had grown too bold. But she soon settled down again. Beyond the jackals there was a second ring around the kill, the hyenas. In no circum- stances, Ker said, would the lions permit them to approach the carcass until they themselves had finished The hyenas, however, were getting at any rate an *hors d'œuvre* in an- other way; every jackal that came away from the kill was immediately set upon and chased across the plain until it dropped the morsel in its mouth – unless of course it suc- ceeded in gulping down the meat in time.

Meanwhile the vultures were arriving. In open country like this it does not take them very long to sight a kill. Each bird, ranging high above the crater, watches the flight of its neighbours, and directly one bird dives, the others follow. They came down in twos and threes, necks thrust forward, and with a frantic beating of their brown wings as they touched the ground. Then they trotted forward and made still another outer ring around the kill.

And so for an hour or more things continued in this way in the bright peaceful sunshine until the lions were gorged at last and moved away. They sat down heavily at a little distance licking their red mouths in the grass. Instantly the hyenas passed through the ring of jackals and set upon the carcass. They fed noisily, snapping and snarling at one another, and like dogs they grabbed the biggest hunks they could get and ran away. It was the turn then of the jackals. The vultures continued to sit and wait; they would wait all night if necessary. In the end nothing would be left except the skin, the hooves, and the wet bones, and upon these the ants would soon be at work.

I found it absorbing too to watch the other animals all through this time. Once the dreadful act of murder had been committed the zebras, the wildebeest, and the antelopes quietly resumed their grazing as though nothing had happened. Now that one of their number had been sacrificed they knew that they were safe for the next two or three days, at all events from these two lions, and all their fear had disappeared. They grazed right up to and around the bloody mess of their dead companion in the same way as a traffic stream will make an island of an accident and continue indifferently on its way.

In other words, there is no real anger in these dramas, and the death of the weak is accepted as part of the natural, unsentimental order of things. If there is anger in animals at all it seems to be reserved for their conflict with human beings, and the occasional fights between evenly matched rivals; the buffalo lunging at his neighbour in the mating season, the mother elephant driving off the lion from her young. And it is the special quality of the Ngorongoro crater that all these things can be observed so easily, almost as though you were sitting at some spectacle in the Roman Colosseum, and against the background of the sun shining so brightly on the close-cropped grass.

Lions, when mating, do not eat as a rule. For a week or more a couple will retire into the long grass or some shady valley and the devotion of the male is extreme : when the female turns her head he turns his too. Wherever she moves he follows. But it is very different when they return to the world again and the female makes a kill. With a forbidding roar the male drives his mate from the prey and she sits waiting a dozen yards or so away until he has finished his meal.

87

When the cubs are born the family groups tend to split up. The males go off to hunt by themselves often in groups of two while the females (sometimes assisted by an unmated lioness who acts as a kind of cubs' nurse) remain with the young.

We camped for four days inside the crater, and then moved west again across the Serengeti Plains. It was exactly the right time of the year to make the journey. The moon was full, and the great January migration of animals was on its long trek out towards Lake Victoria before the rains began. At a guess we must have passed in the space of two days a million gazelle and perhaps half as many wildebeest and zebra. The animals were calving early this year, and it was a marvellous thing to see a young gazelle, hardly a few hours old, get up to trot all day beside its mother. The wildebeest went forward in long columns like squadrons of cavalry, and although apparently no command was given, they kept closing their ranks when gaps occurred. They wheeled together to the left or right, and out on the flanks the sentinels kept their place. The sentinels do not graze like the others as they go along : they keep looking out in all directions across the wide plain, on the watch for lions, no doubt, until they are relieved by some other animal trotting out from the herd to take their place. But how this is organized and who decides just which animal is to go on duty at a certain time no naturalist has yet explained.

CHAPTER FOUR

THE OTHER SIDE OF THE HILL

IT was extraordinary weather. The rain-bird, a small lilac-breasted cuckoo, followed us everywhere. I never did succeed in catching sight of the bird itself, but we woke each morning to the sound of its mournful three-note cry. It went on and on, and it was never wrong. By midday black clouds had piled up over the sun, and in the evening a thunderstorm would burst on top of us. Where normally in January and February we should have been covered in dust, we travelled now in deep black mud with chains on the wheels, and sometimes three hours would go by while we cut down trees and made causeways across the rivers. In all Ker's experience he had never seen mushrooms growing in the bush before, but now we gathered them in hundreds. The animals, I noticed, made no attempt to take cover. Even the lions sat out on the open grass, gazing placidly through the downpour, and they looked as though they might have been carved in stone on the steps of some palace or municipal library. Afterwards when the sun came out the vultures on the flat tops of the acacia trees spread out their wings to dry before they launched themselves again on their endless spirals in the sky.

It was in this rough weather that we splashed and bumped our way up to the village of Loliondo, on the Kenya border, where we were to collect the two policemen who were to protect us from the Mau Mau in the uninhabited country that lay beyond. The police chief, a young Englishman named Michael Leaf, was delighted to see us; the Governor of Tanganyika, he explained, was due to arrive on a tour of inspection on the following day, and it so happened that he had in his force two men of the Masai tribe who were perfectly hopeless on parade. It seemed that any sort of a ceremonial filled these young policemen with horror; they trembled violently, and it was always touch and go as to whether or not they would drop their rifles. These were the two men, Leaf explained cheerfully, whom he had earmarked as our bodyguard; and presently they came marching up the village street towards us. They were in khaki uniform with guns over their shoulders and cartridge belts round their waists, and one of them in particular was of extreme physical beauty. He was very slim and over six foot in height, and it seemed no wonder that the Masai girls came crowding round him when we stopped to make some purchases at the village store. They came up to him softly, their heads shaven, rings of coloured beads sprouting like coral from their ears, their breasts covered with red ochre and grease, and they leaned very carefully over his immaculate tunic to kiss him on the cheek. I was a good deal moved by this scene – this simple and spontaneous adoration of the young Apollo – until Ker explained brusquely that kissing among the Masai has nothing to do with sex; these girls were the young man's sisters and they were merely saying good-bye.

Now finally with the two policemen perched among the other boys on top of the lorry, and Saidi, the head-man, peering out through a trap-door in the roof of our car, we were ready to leave civilization behind. We headed west at first and then turned north across the Kenya border to a place known vaguely on the maps as the Engatapusi Plains.

No one could pretend that our wanderings of the next few weeks came under the heading of exploration, nor was the journey hazardous or uncomfortable in any way; indeed, there was never a thunderstorm so bad that Joseph the cook did not contrive somehow to come up with coffee and eggs in the morning and a four-course dinner at night. Yet there was a certain exhilaration about each day; the simple and perhaps childish pleasure of knowing that no one probably had passed this way before, and that no other human eyes had seen these particular animals roaming across the plain, nor even, possibly, the plain itself. It was the sort of thing that ski-ers feel when they break new snow in the mountains, or sailors in a small boat in a remote sea. In uninhabited country the grass seems fresher and greener, the rocks more ancient, and there is a kind of secrecy in the life that goes on in the hidden glades along the river banks. You break in on the scene with a slight sense of violation, and it is not unpleasant. Every animal turns its head, the birds start up, the crocodile slithers into a pool, and for the moment you, the trespasser, are the master of it all, with a master's instinct for possession; you yourself have found this place, therefore it is yours. It would be intolerable, you feel, if anyone else appeared. Even if he merely stood and looked he would be robbing you of something. I recall one day Ker stopping the car with a jerk and jumping out; he thought he had seen a human footprint on the ground, and we gazed at it with hostility and loathing for quite three minutes until we were certain that it was nothing more than the footstep of an ostrich that had been planted oddly in the dust.

Emotions such as these must have been felt by every explorer and traveller in Africa, and it may seem a little naïve to record them now. But the escape from the city and the roads is more difficult now than it was in the days of Stanley and Livingstone. Even in this lonely pocket of Africa we were not secure from occasional aircraft flying overhead. And so by contrast the sense of isolation and discovery hits one with an extra force. Not once in the past twenty years, I realized, had I really been apart from other people as I was now; and it was an immense satisfaction to see across the scrub a great rounded outcrop of stone, and to bump our way over to it, and then on foot to explore the smooth sides hoping that there would be a cave, a ledge of overhanging boulders, where, untouched for a millennium or so, there still might be a scrawl of red drawings where some Stone Age man had worked with a feather or a pointed bone upon the surface of the rock. The stale cat-smell of leopards which often hangs about such places was quite exciting too. Ker would never let us stray far from the car, for the leopard leaps from above and scalps you with half the speed of light. The fact that the leopard never leapt and there never were any cave-paintings made no difference: I still wanted to explore the next cliff in the next valley, and in the evenings to stroll very quietly down to the river, where, if I parted the reeds carefully enough, I could gaze on a world of reptiles and birds which had not altered much with time.

Then again the converse of all this was true. Coming back to cultivated areas at the end of our trip, I found myself depressed at the tameness of it all, the effect of the dead hand of men and domestic animals on the countryside; the trodden grass, the chopped tree-trunk, the native huts in the clearing, the familiar pattern of cultivated things. We were still a thousand miles away from television and the skyscraper, and these settlements on the edge of the forest were still as primitive as any African travel poster, but to us it was not the same. It was second-hand and it was spoiled. It took me a day or two in a Nairobi hotel to emerge from a deep mist of anti-climax and to discover that there was a certain virtue in the hot bath, the clean shirt, and the iced martini. And then, sliding rapidly down the hill again into civilization, I enjoyed these things very much.

Except for food we did not shoot, and the weather was too grey for photographs; we simply looked. We set off in the car soon after dawn each morning and wandered about for three or four hours with no particular object (and that in itself was a new experience for me: travelling in a car with no idea of *getting* anywhere). Then after lunch and a sleep through the hot hours of the day we set off again in the evening. We dined at eight by a log fire and at half past nine we were in bed. Every three or four days we moved camp to another deserted spot some seventy or eighty miles away.

Outside the Congo and one or two other regions there is virtually no jungle in central Africa. You rarely if ever see a snake, the insects are not nearly so troublesome as they are supposed to be, and you are so high up on the Equator (usually about four thousand feet above sea level) you need three blankets on your bed at night. What you normally see around you is a kind of park. The trees are dotted about at intervals of a hundred yards or so, smooth grass for the most part lies in between, many little streams with trees on their banks meander about, and the whole thing gives you the impression that some landscape artist has been at work. Just occasionally you come on thick scrub on the hillsides, and wide treeless plains that sweep away until they become lost in the blue horizon. The dried-up streams (known as dongas), the park-like plain, and the scrub are the three recurring scenes in this garden, and each contains its own special group of animals. We used to visit them all in turn each day as though we were on a sort of milk-run, gradually working upwards from the valleys across the plains to the rocky hills above, which were the limit of our world for the moment and the only one we cared about.

The lions tended to lurk in the dongas in prides of a dozen or more of all sizes, but they came out to sun themselves on the edge of the plain for an hour or two in the morning, and again in the evening. I suppose we must have seen about a hundred and fifty of them in all, and they alone, of all the wild game (with one unpleasant exception I will come to in a minute), had no fear of us whatsoever. Since they had never been shot at or trapped by poachers we were not regarded as a menace. We found we could drive up to within five or six yards of them, and we elicited nothing more than a casual stare before they turned their heads away or went on sleeping. Sometimes as we moved slowly along in low gear the young lions, out of curiosity, would come loping all round us. We might almost have reached out and stroked their smooth clean yellow backs, and it was odd to think that if you opened the door and stepped out the chances were that you would instantly die. This propinquity was altogether too much for one of our drivers who had not before this ventured far outside Nairobi. He closed his eyes and complained that he felt very cold when the lions came close. There was a canvas blind on the side of the car, and this he used to pull down so that he could obliterate the awful sight of those staring yellow eyes. Then, he explained, he began to warm up again.

For my part, I found the leopards much more alarming than the lions. They seemed to me to be the most beautiful of all the animals, the most lithe and wild. Those that I saw – and you don't see very many – were very pale in colour, almost silver, and their throats were marked with a circular band of black fur patches that hung like a necklace from the base of their round cat-heads. There is a hair-trigger ferocity about the leopards. Each time one lifted one's binoculars for a closer view one was confronted with two green glaring lamps that burned directly into one's own eyes. The pupils had the effect of boring into you. No animal, not even the lion, has such an implacable gaze.

One day we came on an immaculate little female prowling across the wet grass and the behaviour of a group of topi and Grant's gazelle nearby was very strange. They stood and stared at the leopardess with wide straining eyes, and then trotted forward towards her – that is to say towards death. The topi is a fairly mad animal anyway, a large brown gleaming antelope with gun-metal blazes on its legs and an air of continual stage-fright, but these topi outdid themselves. They snorted and snuffled, they stamped with their fore-feet on the turf, and they kept trotting nearer and nearer to the leopardess. Most antelopes prefer to keep a hunting lion or leopard in view and will often approach in this manner, leaving themselving just enough distance to get away in an emergency. But with these topi, and to a lesser extent the Grant's gazelle, it was something more than that. They were in an extremity of fear and they simply could not bring themselves to run away. It almost seemed that some kind of mesmerism was at work upon them, that the dreadful danger had broken down their will, and that something in the nature of a death-wish was luring them on towards the leopardess not thirty yards away. She took no notice either of them or of us for a while, until suddenly the breeze carried our scent in her direction. Then she was up and away like a ballet-dancer and with that the spell was broken: topi and gazelle wheeled together and went galloping down the valley.

Such scenes as these are the heavy drama of the dongas. The comic relief lies just a few yards off on the edge of the plain among the baboons, the mongooses, and the tiny bat-eared foxes. With the possible exception of ostriches, which start their curious pacing-horse run when you are half a mile away, Ker claims that the baboons have sharper eyesight than any other creature on the ground in Africa. He credits them with having eyes the equal of eight-power binoculars. Whether this be so or not, the fact is that the baboons we saw were forever bolting for the cover of the trees long before we could get a close look at them. They ran in packs of fifty or more, the young ones either leaping on their mothers' backs or riding along underneath by clutching the fur of their parents' bellies, and they ran not so much in fear as with an immense boiling anger. Normally all animals flee in silence. But not baboons. It is rather as though you are a policeman breaking up a noisy political meeting. Even before they reach the trees both the young and old are turning their heads and hurling threats, hisses, and screams at you. Once they are in the branches the uproar redoubles, and there is a note of mockery in the cries as you pass beneath. An awful smell of dungeons hangs in the air. All this is mildly embarrassing and even a little annoying – after all, you have done nothing to the baboons except disturb them – and it's much better fun when a leopard, the chief object of the baboons' hatred, is the centre of the abuse. The leopard walks by with a pained look and an elaborate air of paying no attention, but somehow as an act it doesn't quite come off. The leopard has, however, better means of redress than an actor being booed from the gallery; he will return at night when the moon is down, and with one noiseless pounce through the branches will tear some sleeping baboon to pieces.

The other smaller animals, by contrast to these hecklers, are timid and silent in their ways. The tortoises I picked up – and they were lying around like boulders in some places – emitted nothing more than a low despairing hiss. The mongooses that run in families of a score or more sat up on their hindlegs in groups like ninepins when we approached. Then in an undulating scamper they ran in line to their holes in the anthills. They vanished very suddenly, posting themselves like letters in a pillarbox. As for the bat-eared foxes, with their pinched faces and their bright eyes, they made no sound at all that I could hear. Just their heads appeared out of their holes in groups of half a dozen or so, and those enormous rounded ears slowly turned in our direction as we went by like a turning radar screen at an airport.

These small animals are in the main quite harmless, and one grows very fond of them as the days go by, possibly because of their very timidity and unimportance. They were all new to me, and Ker too was delighted when, in this untouched wilderness, we came on rare species which even he had not seen for a long time : the serval cats, the striped hyena (a much handsomer and gentler breed than his spotted counterpart), and klipspringer, who bounds like a goat to the topmost rocks and stands there with his neat feat tucked together and two tiny spikes for horns, peering down at you with demure downward-slanting eyes.

Ker was a little disappointed with the game on the plains, for he expected to see them in great herds after being left so long alone. The unseasonable weather, however, had dispersed them; there was water everywhere to drink and so they had split up into small groups and had wandered far afield. Even so there was hardly a moment as we drove along when more than half a dozen species were not in view; the trotting grey eland, the largest of the antelopes, with the big bulls drawing up in the rear, the kongoni, the fastest of the plains game, the zebras with their round rumps, the roan antelope, which is rare, the waterbuck, which has a hide of light blue-brownish wool, and the impala, which when put to flight will sometimes jump twelve feet clear into the air as he makes his getaway. But the prettiest runners of all were the baby Thomson's gazelles. It is really a bounce more than a run. As soon as they get a little momentum they proceed with all four legs quite stiff, bouncing along from tussock to tussock as though they were treading on springs: a kind of pogo-stick motion which is faster than it looks.

I remarked that all these animals seemed to be in the pink of condition, but Ker said it was always so. No matter how hard the drought or how scarce the feed, the appearance of the game he said never changed. The zebras in particular were always as fat as butter. Age only changed the animals, and sometimes, he said, it was a sad thing to come on an old lion who perhaps had lorded it over a valley for a dozen years or so. Too old to follow the pride any more, too weak to hunt, the beast lies under a bush and somehow keeps itself going by catching unawares some titbit like a small rodent or a guinea hen. Often in their extremity old lions pounce on a porcupine, and that leaves them lame with a mass of quills in their paws. Sometimes, Ker said, he had shot a zebra or a gazelle for an old lion, but that was only postponing things; the hyenas – those same hyenas which once the old monarch had scattered with a roar – were always waiting, and in the end they would polish him off.

The elephants appear to manage old age rather better. It is a fairly common thing in this part of Africa to find an old tusker attended by two or three young guardians or askaris. These young elephants never leave their charge, and every few minutes one can see them raise their trunks to sniff the breeze. At the first smell of danger the warning is sounded – a harsh tearing blast, half a scream and half a roar; the old elephant lumbers off into thick bush and the young ones cover up his rear. They will turn and charge if the hunter follows.

Just now, however, on the Engatapusi Plains, Ker was in no mood to sympathize with elephants. They had used their respite from being hunted to ruin whole stretches of the countryside. Large herds of a hundred or more had been grazing through the scrub, knocking down the best of the trees and sometimes uprooting them altogether. We came on their tracks whenever we reached high ground, and sometimes it looked as though some disease had blasted the forest for a dozen miles around. Often too it was simply wanton destruction; having had their fill of the young leaves and berries from the topmost branches the elephants had gone on knocking down trees just for the hell of it. And now, having done their worst, the herds had quitted the area and had wandered away somewhere to the north.

The scrub now was possessed mainly by the buffaloes, and the giraffes, and both had multiplied enormously. Ker warned me about the buffalo, but I never could bring myself to believe in their ferocity. Buffaloes' eyes are round, black, moist, and soulful, and they gaze at you in an almost human way. The beast itself is huge, of course, and more than once we found ourselves on the edge of a herd of a couple of hundred or so. Quite clearly, had they cared to charge – they had only twenty yards or so to go – we were done for, but they never did. Instead, they stood there with their heads thrown slightly upwards and backwards peering at the car uncertainly until one of their number, usually an old bull at that, would be seized with some dreadful palpitation of the heart and off he would go. When one buffalo runs the rest are bound to follow, and in an instant the ground would be shaking under such a weight of hooves as the directors of western movies might dream about, the dust would fly up, and in a clearing close by some gentle little creature like the oribi or the duiker would lift its head from grazing and gaze at all this bother with genuine surprise.

It was the same with the rhinoceros. It is true that once or twice they began to charge us, their heads well down and with a noise like an express train jumping the points at speed. But always at the last instant they swerved and trotted off into the reeds.

The wild dogs seemed to me to be much more dangerous, and indeed it is a fact that on the appearance of a large pack of them a whole valley or a wide plain will empty itself of animals. Even the lions turn aside and the gazelles of course don't stand a chance. A wild dog hunt is the most merciless thing in the bush. They will single out one animal from a herd and chase it tirelessly in circles until the bitter end. If the leading dogs get tired or dizzy others come on and take their places; and when at last the quarry falls the pack leaps upon the living flesh. One day we came on a batch of six or seven wild dogs on the open plain. Every other living thing had bolted in terror except a herd of wildebeest, and these were utterly demoralized. The dogs had just killed and eaten one of their young, and now the rest of the herd was huddled unnaturally close together a hundred yards away waiting for the next attack. Ker stopped the car and we got out and walked up to the dogs. They were in a hysteria of nervous agitation, their bat-ears twitching, the hair of their hideous botched coats half standing up on end and their jaws sagging open. They made little prancing steps towards us and then slunk sideways back again. It was the atmosphere of a street riot where the crowd – in this case the wildebeest – cowers back to take cover, and the rioters themselves have paused for a moment but are still half mad with excitement and still ready for anything. The dogs ran little circles round us, and I believe that, just conceivably, they might have attacked had we not begun throwing stones at them, a method of defence they found disconcerting since obviously it had not come their way before. In the midst of this the wildebeest seized their chance and in a body bolted for the hills.

Not unnaturally in these surroundings one quickly loses all normal sense of time. The day becomes punctuated not by hours nor by appointments (you have no appointments anyway), but by storms and sunlight and by the chance adventures of your wandering. A week as a period of time has no validity at all, unless perhaps you happen to guess that seven days have gone by from the rising or waning of the moon. One evening we would yank great whiskered mud-fish out of the river, and they were not bad to eat if you soaked them in salt water. The next afternoon we sat and watched the migrating storks come sailing down in front of the storm, and they alighted in such numbers that the acacia trees looked as though they had come out in white blossom, an oddly Japanese effect. These days were not to us Tuesday and Wednesday but the day we caught the mud-fish and the day we watched the storks.

We followed the honey-guide, which is one of those phenomena which you can never quite believe in until you see it with your own eyes. The bird makes a loud twittering over your head until you get up and follow it. From tree to tree it leads you on, twittering madly all the way, and the object of all this is some wild beehive which might be a few hundred yards or a mile or two away. The bird knows that human beings like honey and will open up the hive. Then it can feast on the young larvae of the bees (though some say it is really the wax that the bird is after). I followed a honey-guide for a quarter of a mile one day and then got bored and came back. At once the bird returned and started shrilling at me once more, shrilling so persistently that again I got up and followed. But it was too hot, and I wasn't as keen on honey as all that. I came back again. Saidi did not approve of this at all. If one started a thing, he thought, one ought to go through with it. He added darkly that there was a legend that if you deceived the honey-guide too often it would grow mad and lead you on to a black mamba snake or some equally terrible reptile in the bush.

Saidi and some of the other boys had been with Ker for more than twenty years, and it was always a pleasant thing to watch them working in the bush. They could set up camp with astonishing speed; within an hour the tents were up, hot water was in the canvas bath, the dinner-table was laid, and the dinner itself was cooking on a long log fire of red-hot ashes. They had done it all a thousand times before, and no one shouted or got excited. One man washed and ironed the laundry, another cut up the meat and hung it by a rope over a high branch beyond the reach of leopards, others inflated the rubber mattresses, set out the drinks, and refuelled the vehicles for the following day. It was all very grand, and for the client very relaxing. To have no responsibility, that was the delightful part of it, simply to let the days go by knowing that if the truck got stuck again in the next river Saidi and the other boys would get it out, and that Ker was checking on the strange animal noises around the camp at night, and that someone was sure to bring you your malaria pill at the right time in the morning.

There was an anachronistic note in all this. One felt like a feudal baron who had somehow got himself attached to a travelling circus. God knows what the boys thought of the clients they had taken out on so many safaris, and judging from Ker's reminiscences they had coped with some pretty odd ones at times. All I can say is that I was confronted with an apparently inexhaustible good humour, and I daresay it would have been the same if I had been a film star or a sporting millionaire, if I had bolted when the rhinoceros charged or had stood my ground manfully behind Ker and his rifle.

Even on this non-shooting safari Ker's rifle very much dominated the proceedings. To the boys it was the symbol of the whole expedition : his prowess as a marksman established their own place in the world, and there was always a noticeable quickening of interest among them on those days when he went out to shoot for meat. On this trip Ker used eight bullets and made eight kills : a zebra, two kongoni, a topi, three Thomson's gazelle, and a duck. It was almost a surgical thing, and I think I know why he hated it. He could not miss. From the moment he picked out from the herd the buck he wanted (never a female) the animal had only a few minutes to live. He would stop the car and survey the quarry for a moment through his binoculars. Then with no word spoken – nothing said about the direction of the wind, the cover, or the light – he and Saidi got out and walked away in single file. Saidi was always dressed in immaculate khaki with a turban on his head, Ker in green corduroy, and I used to watch these two figures until they were merely two upright dots of colour in the distance. The herd watched too, and then suddenly the green figure dropped to the ground and the rifle was raised. It was all over in the space of two seconds : the soft cough of the explosion, the herd bolting, and the one animal standing staggering for a moment before it fell to the ground. Even before Saidi had finished quartering the carcase the herd – or perhaps other herds – would come grazing back again, and except for the approaching vultures the whole incident passed out of existence as though it had never happened. It seemed strange that a tragedy could occur with such silence and such dispatch. Killing without passion leaves a gap in the mind, and the very expertise of the affair gave one a sense of anti-climax.

Ker usually shot from about two hundred yards away, and his bullet went straight through the heart. His killing of the duck, however, was really spectacular. I had seen this duck, a knob-bill and one of a pair, on a small lake one evening, and had remarked that it would be nice to have roast duck for dinner. Ker explained that with the sort of big-game bullets he was using the duck would disintegrate into thin air, feathers and all. Nevertheless, he got up early the next morning and shot the bird – precisely through the neck. Two nights later the cook did us up a dinner of mushrooms on toast, duck soup, fried mud-fish, and steaks of Thomson's gazelle. I too began to reverence Ker's rifle after that. Like the zebras, we were as fat as butter when early in February we left our retreat and turned towards the north on the last stage of the safari.

It took us three days to get back to the settled areas, three days of crossing over rivers and digging the vehicles out of the mud, and then, keeping to the eastern rim of the Great Rift Valley, we drove for three hundred miles into the Northern Frontier District of Kenya, on the Abyssinian border. We made camp on the banks of the Uaso Nyiro River at the edge of the Marsabit reserve.

Now everything was changed. Where all before had been wet and green and empty of human beings (not even the Mau Mau had appeared) we were now surrounded by tribesmen, and the dry land stretched away into semi-deserts and weird bare rocky mountains. It was the sort of difference that one discovers between Scotland and the south of Spain, between the remoter parts of Vermont and New Mexico. We were now down to 2,500 feet above sea level, and there was a solid steady warmth in the air. The rain-bird vanished, and in its place bright fantastic insects flew through the air.

Not unnaturally, since we had been so long away on our own, it was the local tribesmen who first took my eye. This was the territory of the frizzy-haired Somalis who worship Mohammed, of other tribes who are supposed to be the ugliest people in Africa (though for my money the pygmies in the Congo leave them far behind), and of the Samburu, who are a tall fine slender people with something of the ancient Egyptians about them. Like the Masai, the Samburu are a nomadic cattle-grazing people who have managed fairly successfully to keep modern civilization at bay. They load their women with bead necklaces and coiled wire bracelets by the hundredweight, and the men are mighty walkers; they think nothing of covering forty miles in a day. It is not easy to convey the peculiar attractiveness of the Hamitic tribes. There is very little of the Negro about them; their skin tends to be more coffee-coloured than black and their features have a European cast. They hold themselves with a splendid air of independence and although they may live in squalid, foul-smelling huts, they account white men as no more than equal.

These people, the Samburu, the Gallas, and others who migrated from the north into central Africa several centuries ago, have fascinated explorers from the earliest times; even the great Samuel Baker, an austere man – and one can use the word austere here with a Victorian emphasis – was moved to unusual prose by the Galla women whom he saw when he was making his way down from Abyssinia to the Great Rift.

'On my return to camp,' he wrote, 'I visited the establishments of the various slave merchants: they were arranged under large tents of matting, and contained many young girls of extreme beauty, ranging from nine to seventeen years of age. These lovely captives, of a rich brown tint, with delicately formed features, and eyes like those of the gazelle, were natives of the Galla, on the borders of Abyssinia, from which country they were brought by Abyssinian traders to be sold for the Turkish harems. Although beautiful, these girls are useless for hard labour; they quickly fade away and die unless kindly treated. They are the Venuses of that country, and not only are their faces and figures perfection, but they become extremely attached to those who show them kindness, and they make good and faithful wives. There is something peculiarly captivating in the natural grace and softness of these young beauties, whose hearts quickly respond to those warmer feelings of love that are seldom known among the sterner and coarser tribes. Their forms are peculiarly elegant and graceful – the hands and feet are exquisitely delicate : the nose is slightly aquiline, the nostrils large and finely-shaped; the hair is black and glossy, reaching to about the middle of the back, but rather coarse in texture. These girls, although natives of Galla, invariably call themselves Abyssinians and are generally known under that denomination. They are exceedingly proud and high-spirited and are remarkably quick at learning. At Khartoum several of the Europeans of high standing have married these charming ladies, who have invariably rewarded their husbands by great affection and devotion. The price of one of these beauties at Gallabat was from twenty-five to forty dollars.'

This was in 1862. I myself saw no woman in the northern districts of Kenya who would quite measure up to Baker's description, although indeed there was a group of young girls who used to bathe each day, beads and all, in the river below our camp. On the other hand, Ker assured me slavery still exists. He himself, as an officer on patrol in these areas during the last war, had seen captives being led away in chains, and even at present, he said, Abyssinian slave traders made raids down into Kenya in the vicinity of Lake Rudolf. The buying and selling of wives also goes on, and quite legally; Ker had recently bought a new wife for one of his boys who had been with him a long time.

As for the countryside itself – this huge area which stretches across Italian Somaliland to Lake Rudolf and the borders of Uganda – very little has happened to change it since Baker's day. For some reason the animals here, like the inhabitants, are quite different from those in the rest of Africa. Most of them, I soon saw, were smaller than those we had come across in the south, and indeed the dik dik, the smallest antelope of all, had here shrunk to the size of a little whippet. The impala was a duller shade of caramel, and he had a much greater spread of horns. The male' ostriches were quite unlike the somewhat shaggy birds that had paced away from us in Tanganyika; here their feathers were a magnificent blue-black, and even their usually bald necks and legs were feathered. The baboons, perhaps because they were used to seeing the Samburu in the bush, were much more friendly, and the zebra was so different as to be almost another beast: the broad zigzag stripes had been replaced by thin grey bands that ran directly round the animal's body, and they were spaced so solidly together that from a distance it looked as though the coat was a solid block of grey. This northern species is the Grevy zebra, and although its rump is small it is a larger animal than the common variety. It is equipped with huge ears, and is much tamer; it can be broken into harness.

But it was the giraffe that presented the greatest difference of all. Here on these dry plains, and only here, the reticulated giraffe appears. Its skin is not a series of surrealist blotches but a very definitely marked network of lines with patches of dark chocolate colour in between: an effect such as you get with a crazy pavement. Giraffes are gentle creatures, and there is something virginal and modest about them all; but this particular breed in the north is so slim and pretty that it is the very essence of the *jeune fille*. They look at you timidly over the tops of the bushes, keeping just their heads in sight, like schoolgirls peeping out of a dormitory window. I never got close enough to make quite certain that they have long curling eyelashes, but apparently it is so, and however any sportsman could ever want to shoot so inoffensive and charming a beast is something that must pass any normal understanding.

I used to watch all these animals come down to the Uaso Nyiro in the afternoon, and this perhaps is the best of Africa : to sit very quietly on the banks of a river through the last hot hours of the day and watch (as one might watch from a café chair in the Champs-Élysées) the local life go by. For quite long periods nothing happens. The crocodile (very pale green ones up here) slithers off the sandbank and leaves the river a blank. You are being watched, you know, from all around, and from the branches up above, by many different eyes, and it's just a matter of sitting still until the birds and animals are reassured that you are not dangerous. This is not always the easiest thing in the world to do when wayward biting ants crawl up inside your shirt, but you manage it somehow, and gradually you become an accepted part of the scene along the river; you breathe with it, you vibrate, as it were, at the right slow tempo. Then anything can happen.

I was much taken one day by a sick elephant. He was standing there quite alone, ankle-deep in the muddy water in the middle of the river, his trunk curling just an inch or two above the surface, and for a good fifteen minutes he never moved at all. He made no attempt to drink or wash himself. The river flowed down on him, hornbills and bright kingfishers swooped past, baboons in dozens ran past on either bank, and tall palms and acacia trees rose overhead. But none of it was any good to this elephant. It may have been that he was suffering from toothache or some gargantuan stomach disorder, and quite clearly life for him was hell. He stood there ruminating, merely enduring existence, until at last some dull hope made him think that he would feel better if he got back to the bank; and then he painfully pulled himself up through the reeds on to the high ground on the opposite side. He disappeared slowly through the bushes, and it was unnatural that he was not even bothering to feed.

It seemed a little ruthless of the rest of the herd to have abandoned this sad old sack like this, especially as the herd, I knew, was in particularly good condition. Ker and I had been following it for several days. There were about forty elephants in all, mostly females and young, and when they came down to the river one evening it was quite a sporting event. They did not hurry to the water – and now that I come to think of it I have never seen an African elephant hurry anywhere. When it is not hunted or molested it is the least bothered of animals. It knows that all in good time it will reach the river, and so it pauses on the bank and proceeds in the most maddeningly deliberate way to stuff a few extra hundredweight of grass and green leaves into its mouth. The young ones are excessively well behaved. It may have been several days since they have drunk or bathed, but they make no effort to chivvy their parents on. They stand beside their mothers stolidly feeding on the grass and peering into space with a curious inward look as though they are savouring every mouthful, morsel by morsel, as it goes down.

At last after half an hour or so some old bull makes a move. He turns, almost as if by an afterthought, and gazes with his brown eye at the water: 'Ah, the river!' and then he lowers himself with immense care down the bank. This is the signal for the others to follow, not hurriedly of course, and certainly not with any unseemly noise or excitement, but just gently and quietly in groups of two or three. Then finally the dignified calm is broken, and it is even a little difficult for an observer to keep pace with the proceedings. The old bull is down in midstream, his legs threshing in the air, his head underneath, and just his trunk appearing like a periscope above the surface. Two young couples have started some sort of game, whether through love or just high spirits it is impossible to say, but it involves a good deal of splashing about and intertwining of their trunks. Their tusks clang loudly when they collide, and they continue strenuously with this game until some senior elephant happens to wade by. Then they step politely aside until he has passed before they resume the game again. The dowagers of the herd, meanwhile, have found an excellent high muddy bank, and with immense rumbles of satisfaction they slowly rub their backs along it: back and forth, back and forth, perhaps fifty times in all. The massage concludes with a roll in the grass and a mud-slinging match. Elephants dearly like a good coating of mud on their hides to keep the flies at bay, and so now they gather up the good black fruity mixture from the bottom of the river and squirt it backward through their trunks along their flanks, first this side, then the other, and then a lateral shot along the belly underneath. With one trunk you can cover a lot of territory once you have got into a regular pendulum motion.

In the midst of all this the baby elephants hardly know what to do: to have a scratch along the bank? To roll in the grass? To try the old man's gimmick of putting his head under-water and breathing through his trunk? Or play this delightful game of hurling mud about? In the end they run to and fro from one thing to the other, and it is not until their mothers call them that they will stand still at last and quietly take their last long drink before they leave the river. Eventually, at some sign which is understood among themselves, the herd with one accord wades over to the opposite bank, hauls itself on to dry land and begins feeding again. One by one the great grey rumps vanish into the scrub. For a while then there is no sound at all, nothing but the muddy water rippling and folding over on itself in the shallows until, very softly, the giraffes come questing through the trees to take their turn to drink.

I watched this scene for nearly three hours one day, and still it was not enough. It is always like this once you get into the remote parts of Africa. You do not want to change or improve anything. You simply want to watch and see and then to go on again, to cross the borders into Abyssinia, to climb the flat-topped mountain in the distance, to find another river and another herd of elephants. You can never really have enough.

CHAPTER FIVE

THE POISONED ARROW

NOBODY knows how many wild animals have been killed in British East Africa since the first white men penetrated into the interior just on a hundred years ago, but it must be many millions. Richard Burton, who in 1856 was one of the earliest explorers to find his way into Tanganyika, speaks of coming across many tribesmen with 'full-sized bows and sheaths of grinded arrows whose black barbs and necks showed a fresh layer of poison', and he goes on to say, 'Elephants are numerous in this country; every forest is filled with deep traps, and during the droughty seasons many are found dead in the jungle.' At that time the ivory trade was tied up with the slave traffic, and it was a very profitable business indeed; the slaves acted as porters, each man carrying at least one tusk on the long journey down to the coast on the Indian Ocean, and at Mombasa both slaves and tusks were sold together.

Yet there was still no really widespread destruction of the wild game; neither the Arab traders nor the Africans themselves wasted their ammunition on anything less valuable than an elephant unless they were hungry or in danger, and so there was a sort of coexistence between human beings and animals and there was room enough for everyone to live. Most Africans in any case were much more interested in fighting one another rather than wild beasts, and the Masai tribe, which was the most warlike of the lot, were scarcely hunters at all; they had their own herds of domestic cattle which satisfied nearly all their needs.

When Joseph Thomson arrived in Tanganyika twenty-five years after Burton he was still able to see remarkable quantities of game. Thomson headed north-westwards from Mombasa through the Masai country, and his description of what he saw still has a glow of wonder and excitement about it.

'There,' he wrote, 'towards the base of Kilimanjaro, are three great herds of buffalo slowly and leisurely moving up from the lower grazing grounds to the shelter of the forest for their daily snooze and rumination in its gloomy depths. Farther out on the plains enormous numbers of the harmless but fierce-looking wildebeest continue their grazing, some erratic members of the herd gambolling and galloping about, with waving tail and strange uncouth movements. Mixed with these are to be seen companies of that loveliest of all large game, the zebra, conspicuous in their beautiful striped skin – here marching with stately step, with heads bent down, there enjoying themselves by kicking their heels in mid-air or running open-mouthed in mimic flight, anon standing as if transfixed, with heads erect and projecting ears, watching the caravan pass. But these are not all. Look! Down in that grassy bottom there are several specimens of the great, unwieldy rhinoceros, with horns stuck on their noses in a most offensive and pugnacious manner. Over that ridge a troop of ostriches are scudding away out of reach of danger, defying pursuit, and too wary for the stalker. See how numerous are the herds of hartebeest; and notice the graceful pallah (impala) springing into mid-air with great bounds, as if in pure enjoyment of existence. There also, among the tall reeds near the marsh, you perceive the dignified waterbuck, in twos and threes, leisurely cropping the dewy grass. The warthog, disturbed at his morning's feast, clears off in a bee-line with tail erect, and with a steady military trot, truly comical. These do not exhaust the list, for there are many other species of game. Turn in whatever direction you please, they are to be seen in astonishing numbers, and so rarely hunted, that unconcernedly they stand and stare at us, within gunshot.

'Look now further ahead. Near a dark line of trees which conspicuously mark out the course of the Ngaro N'Erobi (cold stream) in the treeless expanse around, you observe in the clear morning air columns of curling smoke, and from the vicinity strange long dark lines are seen to emerge like the ranks of an advancing army. The smoke marks the kraals of the Masai and the advancing lines are their cattle moving towards the pasture-ground.'

This was in 1882. Soon afterwards firearms began to find their way into the interior, and the process of killing was greatly accelerated. Then at the turn of the century slavery was abolished (though it lingered on in Zanzibar for a few more years), and this made it all the more necessary for the traders to make good their lost business in slaves by getting more ivory. At the same time they developed a number of sidelines in the sale of hides, rhinoceros horn, and *biltong*, which is simply meat that has been cut into strips and laid out in the air to dry.

It is, of course, illegal to trap or shoot wild animals except under licence, but this doesn't seem to have made much difference to the steady extermination of what is left of the great herds which once used to roam all through Kenya and Tanganyika. Poaching of the big game reserves has developed into an organized business, and it is estimated that there are as many as a hundred rings or gangs of traders involved in it.

I first became interested in these questions when I was in Kenya early in 1956, and I spent some weeks trying to discover just how the poaching was done and why it wasn't stopped. At the outset it seemed to be a simple sort of inquiry to make, but as time went on I discovered that it was anything *but* simple. Nothing ever is in Africa; sooner or later every issue tends to get bedevilled by strong local feelings, and the very primitiveness of Africa itself is the death of an easy logic. And this applies with particular force to this matter of the vanishing wild animals.

In Nairobi the officials in the game department were very gloomy. 'If something isn't done soon,' one of them said, 'there won't be a wild animal larger than a rabbit left alive in Africa. Except of course in the game reserves. But then the reserves themselves are in danger of being broken up.'

'Then why isn't something done?'

'Not enough game rangers and no money to employ any more. And the law against poaching is ridiculously weak.'

'Then why not change the law?'

'A lot of people don't want to change the law. They regard wild animals as vermin and they say that they are bound to be exterminated anyway because the land is wanted for agriculture and domestic stock.'

I was armed with a booklet of official statistics which stated that the tourist trade was worth about £6 million to East Africa every year – quite an important item in this limited economy – and I quoted this. 'Surely,' I said, 'people don't come to Africa to see the cities and the factories and the farms. They want to see the buffaloes and the elephants.'

'True enough. But just try and persuade the settlers about this. All they are interested in is the fact that a herd of elephant came across their land last month and trampled their crops. As for the Africans, they have always hunted animals. It is the instinctive thing for them to do.'

And so the argument went on and it stirred up some odd scraps of information which were new to me: the fact, for example, that the great majority of Africans have never seen an elephant or a buffalo. Big game as a rule keeps well away from the settled areas, and the average African child is probably much more ignorant about wild life than any schoolboy or girl in London or New York. Consequently there is very little interest in the local fauna and the chances of persuading the tribesmen to preserve it on humanitarian or aesthetic or even economic grounds are not very bright. This is what makes the British officials so despondent about the future of the game parks; presumably they will all have to be handed over to purely African governments one day.

Another man to whom I talked in Nairobi was a member of the local wild life society which is fighting a lively rearguard action for the animals' survival. He produced a quotation from Mark Twain – the one about the lack of money being the root of all evil. 'Down in Mombasa,' he said,

Quiet, aldermanic dignity

(a) The calves kept straying out through their mothers' legs

(b) *Une jolie laide:* the warthog

(a) The kudu bull and his wives

(b) The power of a great locomotive: the rhinoceros

(a) The leopard leaps from above

(b) Death of the weak

(a) Cheetahs on a kill

(b) The hyena's guilty look

(a) The lioness brakes as it sees the impala

(b) An impala jumps . . .

(a) ... and gets clear away

(b) But the second impala is seized by the lioness

(b) The marabou with his hard
hangman's eye

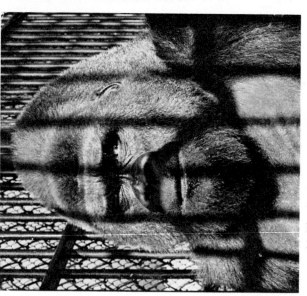

(a) The dignity and majesty of prophets:
the gorilla in captivity

8

The ruffians lie sleeping in the sun's blaze

9

(b) A serval kitten

(a) The waterbuck

(a) No living creature runs like the giraffe

(b) Baboons

(a) Wildebeeste: the migration on the Serengeti Plains

(b) Vultures on a kill

(c) Turkana fishermen on Lake Rudolf

Masai tribesman

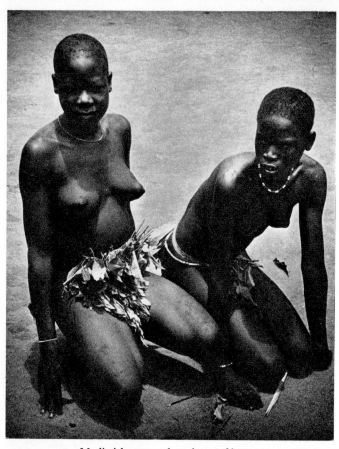
Madi girls wear only a clump of leaves

Madi girls at school

Tall, fine, slender people: the Samburu

'ivory goes for around £1 a lb., and a good pair of tusks will weigh up to 160 lb. The traders there want the stuff for small carved figures and tourist souvenirs, and they can never get enough of it. Rhinoceros horn is exported to China where it is sold in powdered form as an aphrodisiac, and *that* fetches up to £4 a lb. On a mature beast the two horns might weigh ten lb. Then there is crocodile skin which is used for making shoes and bags. The present price for it is around seven shillings and sixpence or a dollar an inch – an inch strip taken across the belly. This money represents wealth in this country, and you are not going to keep the traders or the tribesmen away from it with a handful of game wardens.'

Most of the tribesmen, however, kill animals because they want meat, either to eat themselves while it is fresh or to dry out and sell as *biltong*. All the usual devices are employed: the pit into which it is intended that the animal will fall and impale itself on a spike: shooting with cheap home-made guns (there are said to be a hundred thousand of them at least in East Africa), and very often they wound without killing; and the snares. These snares are wire nooses which are set on the tracks which the animals normally use on their passage to and from the waterholes. If no such tracks exist the hunter will erect a brush fence with perhaps half a dozen gaps in it, and once the animals have grown accustomed to using these gaps the nooses are set there, quite big nooses, big enough to strangle a wildebeest or a giraffe.

There is much wastage in this business. Often the hunter is simply interested in getting a meal for himself and his family, and when one beast is caught he is content. But he does not bother to remove the other four or five snares, and each of them will eventually catch an animal of some kind which is left to rot, and to be eaten by the hyenas and the vultures. Even if the trapped animal succeeds in breaking away, its death is very likely because the wire trailing around its neck will eat into its skin and probably cause a painful and mortal wound.

But it is the use of nets which is really devastating. These nets are set up like a fence for as much as a mile or more across the open countryside, and the herds of zebras, wildebeest, giraffe, and gazelle, in fact any game that comes to hand, are driven into them. In their fright the animals quickly become entangled, and then it is an easy matter to dispatch them with a spear or a knife. Things might not be too bad if the animals were always killed outright, but quite often in a big drive the poachers have a problem in keeping the meat fresh until they are ready to use it. They solve this by hamstringing the beasts; a nick in the tendons on one of the hind-legs will ensure that they will not stray very far. Recently a Nairobi game-ranger came across forty zebra that had been dealt with in this way; some were already dead of thirst and hunger, some were lying down and dying, and others still had enough strength to hobble about for a few more days on three legs.

Here again there is great wastage, especially in the case of the giraffe and the wildebeest, which are not often hunted for their meat or skins at all; the giraffe are killed because their tails provide a tough twine which is useful for making spears and arrows, while the wildebeest tail is still more valuable since it can be sold down in Mombasa as a fly-switch. Once the tail has been chopped off the rest of the carcass is abandoned.

It is the elephant, however, which offers the really great prize to the poaching gangs, and in recent years they have been particularly concentrating upon the Tsavo Park, a big stretch of uninhabited bush which lies just inside the Kenya border to the east of Kilimanjaro. I drove down there one warm April day just as the rains were breaking, and spent a weekend with David Sheldrick, the game warden. Sheldrick was an expert about elephant poaching; he was actually engaged in a private war against the poaching gangs, and to have heard him discourse on the subject was a fascinating experience.

The Wakamba and the Waliangulu tribes appeared to be the main elephant hunters, and their chief weapons are those same poisoned arrows which Burton noticed a century ago. The poison is taken from a local tree called the *acokanthera frisiorum*, and in all Africa, a land of venomous serpents and plants, there is nothing quite so virulent. The recipe for the preparation of the mixture has a distinctly medieval sound. First small twigs and leaves are gathered from the tree, and with a series of successive boilings over eight or nine days the sap is reduced to a substance which smells like liquorice and has the colour and consistency of pitch. Sometimes, so the story goes, a live shrew is thrown into the brew to give it extra pungency. There is no known antidote to this poison (Sheldrick would not let me touch a pot of the stuff he had in his office); it kills in ten or fifteen minutes. You can usually recognize an *acokanthera frisiorum* in the bush; it looks somewhat like an olive and often there are numbers of insects and small rodents lying dead at the foot of the tree.

In every Wakamba village there is probably a small factory for the manufacture of the poison; it is done up in small packets, each packet just enough for one arrow, and sold to the poachers at sixpence a time. The tribesmen go to great trouble over the construction of their bows and arrows: just the right kind of vulture feather must be fixed to the arrow, and the bowstring must be made of some such bizarre material as the intestine of a giraffe. Each tribe has its own notions about the size and resilience of the bow, and each man has his own sign on the arrowhead so that there will be no dispute as to which arrow has killed which elephant. The poison is carefully pasted round the shaft of the arrowhead and then covered with a tape made of fibre; it deteriorates very quickly if it is exposed to the air, especially in cold weather. This tape is taken off just before the arrow is used, and the arrowhead itself becomes detached from the shaft directly it strikes, so that it will penetrate deeply into the quarry. Armed with these formidable weapons, the poachers set off in batches of anything up to fifty men into the depth of the Tsavo Park.

In the dry weather the main hunting grounds are around the waterholes where the elephants come to bathe and drink during the hot midday hours, and the technique of the poachers is simple: they secrete themselves on some high rock above the water and shoot from a distance of twenty or thirty yards. At once there is an immense commotion. The wounded beast – and it is customary of course to concentrate on the elephant with the largest tusks – goes crashing off into the bush with the rest of the herd stampeding around him. When he falls and lies threshing about on the ground the other elephants come back to help him. They thrust their trunks under his huge bulk and try to get him to his feet again. Then when he lies still they stand uncertainly for a while, smelling at the blood on the dead animal's hide and recoiling from it, until at last they seem to realize that there is nothing to be done. And then they turn hopelessly away.

Occasionally a wounded elephant will rush off so far into the forest that he eludes the poachers, though death of course is bound to find him in the end. Then an extraordinary thing sometimes happens. The other elephants will descend on the dead beast and tear out its tusks, afterwards shattering them to pieces on the rocks and boulders they happen to find nearby. Sheldrick hesitated to explain this by saying that the elephants know that they are being hunted for their tusks, and are determined to deprive their tormentors of their booty. But he knew of no other explanation to give.

For the most part, however, the poachers soon find the animals they have shot, and then it is only a matter of a few minutes to chop off the tusks and continue on their way again. And thus, working from waterhole to waterhole, the gang may continue for days or even weeks on end.

When a sufficient quantity of ivory is gathered, a messenger is sent to one of the illegal ivory traders in Mombasa fixing a rendezvous at some convenient but lonely spot on the Mombasa–Nairobi road. The trader, usually an Indian, drives up quite openly in the daylight in a truck or an ordinary touring car, but when he stops he takes the precaution of lifting up the bonnet. The idea of this is to give the impression that he has stopped because of engine trouble, and if another car should chance to come by he waves it on, saying that he is in no real difficulty, just a little trouble with the fan belt or the ignition or some other minor thing. Then directly the other car is gone the poachers emerge from the bush. The deal is quickly made; the price the trader pays is, of course, a great deal lower than the market price in Mombasa, but the poachers are simple people and they are not in a very good position to argue. Then the tusks are thrown into the back of the truck and are covered with a sheet of tarpaulin. An hour or two later the trader is back in Mombasa.

Even here he has very little difficulty in getting rid of his illegal goods. A great deal of ivory that has been obtained under licence goes through the Mombasa market in a perfectly legal way, and it is almost impossible for the government inspectors to spot a pair of tusks that has come from the poachers, especially when it has been cut up into short lengths. Quite a large part of the illegal ivory is exported, and it is a simple matter for the traders to hide the tusks in bales of cotton or in casks of buffalo-milk butter, and these are loaded in hundreds aboard the Arab dhows which ply across the Indian Ocean to Zanzibar, Arabia, and India. Rhinoceros horn, being smaller (it is not actually horn, but hair matted together and as hard as iron), is even easier to disguise. The customs officials on the coast know all about these practices but they say they have not the staff to open every barrel and bale of cloth that comes down to the docks; and in fact they seldom catch anybody. And so from month to month the trade goes on. To keep it going about 600 elephants and 200 rhinoceroses are killed every year, and this in the area of the Tsavo Park alone.

Sheldrick organized a small private army of African game wardens to fight the poachers inside the park. For the most part these men were tough and disciplined characters brought down from the far north of Kenya, and they had no love for the Wakamba and Waliangulu tribesmen. They fought in a way that ought to endear them to any school-boy's heart. The patrols went out in batches of about eight men, and they were armed with rifles, a supply of food, and a radio. They knew the habits of the poaching gangs and the areas in which they were most likely to work, and they stalked them silently through the bush, sometimes for days or even weeks. From time to time Sheldrick got information which he could relay to his men over the radio, and latterly he had the use of a spotting aircraft but for the most part the patrols used the ordinary native lore or the bush. They watched the vultures; they picked up the tracks of the poachers in the sand. They laid ambushes beside the water-holes. Quite unknown to the outside world many desperate little battles have been fought in the Tsavo Park.

As a rule the patrols attacked by night. At a given signal they rushed out from their hiding places hoping to catch the poachers asleep on the ground, and usually the poachers did not put up much of a fight. Those who failed to get away (and they had a habit of sleeping under separate trees so that they could escape more easily if they were surprised) were very quickly overwhelmed by a few quick blows. Then the handcuffs were snapped on and they were marched away. Sometimes, however, there was a skirmish – the rifle against the poisoned arrow – and it was not al-ways the rangers who won.

In one year alone Sheldrick made some thirty or forty arrests, but he knew that he was still a long way from getting the upper hand. The forest is vast and his forces are much too small to cover it all. Then, too, imprisonment is not much of a deterrent to the poachers. In Kenya the maximum penalty for killing an elephant is only six months, and to an African gaol is not such a terrible place. With the more sophisticated Indian trader, of course, it is a different matter; he doesn't like gaol at all, but Indian traders have money and can summon up clouds of wit-nesses. 'It's not much use,' Sheldrick said, 'to offer a reformed poacher £50 to give evidence for us; the trader can give him £100 or more to keep quiet.'

I asked why the use of poisoned arrows was not banned by the government, and was told that the matter was being considered and steps had already been taken in Kenya. Yet even here there were difficulties. The tribesmen have always used poisoned arrows; it is their traditional way of obtaining food and many of them are not professional poachers. They hunt quite legitimately outside the parks, and it is argued that it would be wrong to take away their livelihood. Then too there is always the possibility that if you impose harsher penalties on the poachers you will antagonize the tribes.

This last – the antagonizing of the tribes – is the real issue. The Mau Mau rebellion in Kenya is very recent, and no one wants it to flare up again down here in southern Kenya and Tanganyika among the other tribes – especially the Masai.

It is with this mention of the word Masai that one finally reaches the heart of the matter, for the poaching problem, one soon discovers, is only part of the story, and perhaps not even the most important part; in the long run the Masai may be even more fatal to the wild game. You hear about the Masai almost from the first moment you arrive in East Africa. One is either for them or against them, and an endless controversy rages over the tribe. The Masai number about 55,000 in all, and they are by some way the most interesting and certainly the most spectacular people in all black Africa. As a tribe they have done the thing that practically no other Africans have succeeded in doing: they have rejected the twentieth century and the white man's world and have, instead, remained loyal to their ancient tribal customs.

It's quite a startling thing when you first meet a Masai warrior. He is not like an African at all. He stands six feet tall, a slim hipless figure with a rust-coloured cloak hanging over one shoulder and a broad-bladed spear in his hand. His face is thin with very high cheek-bones, his eyes are two narrow mongolian slits, and no man on this earth, not even a Red Indian chieftain, can look at you with so much arrogance and fierce pride.

To Thomson and the other pioneers who first penetrated into their tribal areas the Masai were a holy terror. If the warriors were not fighting one another or raiding the neighbouring tribes – and they usually were – they took a delight in falling upon these white intruders, and if they felt like it they murdered them. Since those days the Masai have become a good deal less aggressive with strangers, but in almost all other respects they have remained the same.

They never wash. At certain times they streak their faces with coloured grease and dirt, and braid their hair so as to give it the appearance of a mop. The lobes of their ears are pierced and stretched fantastically with heavy ornaments. They drink deeply of the local beer and some of their tribal ceremonies are said to be barbaric. Yet none of this in any way disturbs the Masai's absolute conviction that he is an aristocrat, a member of a superior race. He disdains all forms of trade and ordinary labour – even his weapons are made for him by inferior tribes – and he is too a mighty man in slow portentous rhetorical argument, just as he is in lion killing, and every young man is supposed to kill at least one lion alone and only with his spear.

The women don't count for much in the social organization of the tribe; they are promiscuous both before and after marriage, and are bought and sold like so much livestock. But from birth the men are fixed in a rigid and patrician system. In turn they enter each of the three main tribal groups, the adolescents, the warriors, and the elders. Each of these groups appoints a leader who has a hand in the inner councils of the tribe, and in addition to these, dominating the race but not actually leading it, are the libans, the medicine-men who are in touch with the mystical divine being who lives, some believe, on the topmost snowy crest of Kilimanjaro.

The Masai is a nomad and he lives by grazing cattle. Cattle are his wealth, his social standing, and his food. Having milked his cows he punctures a vein in their necks so that he can draw off a quantity of blood to be added to the milk, and this, together with maize, is his staple diet. To ensure that there is an adequate supply of this exotic nourishment the Masai drive great herds of cattle across the open plains of Kenya and Tanganyika, and they are constantly adding to their stock. In recent years the herds in some parts have increased beyond all calculation; where once a family might have got along on thirty beasts they now possess three hundred. As cattle they may be poor specimens and diseased as well, but this does not matter, they take the place of currency; it is their numbers that count in all matters of bartering, including the bartering for a bride. And so, inevitably, the Masai are forced to spread further and further afield in search of water and fresh grazing in order to keep their swollen herds alive. This is where the conflict comes in between the tribe and the people who want to preserve what is left of the wild game, since clearly there is not enough grazing and water to go round; eventually either the wild animals or the Masai herds will have to go.

The problem is not really a local one since the Masai spread over such a large area of East Africa, but it so happens that the Serengeti Park is involved, and the Serengeti has been a name to conjure with in East Africa in recent years. If one wanted to stir up conversation anywhere in Kenya or Tanganyika one simply mentioned the Serengeti question and then sat back and listened.

I had heard a good deal about this place in Nairobi and elsewhere when I first arrived in Kenya. The Serengeti, I was told, supported the last great concentration of wild animals left alive in the world. Here and only here in all Africa could one find such masses of big game as Thomson had seen in 1882. It is a large park covering roughly 6,000 square miles just inside the northern borders of Tanganyika, and it reaches all the way from the shores of Lake Victoria to the Ngorongoro Crater, which is almost within sight of Kilimanjaro. The importance of this particular stretch of country is that the animals use it as a migration route; as soon as the wet season ends they move eastwards from Lake Victoria in tens of thousands, breeding and pasturing as they go along, and then when the rains begin again they turn back towards the lake. To see these hordes in motion is one of the most arresting sights in Africa.

And now the Masai had entered the scene; some five thousand tribesmen were living in the park, and they had with them about a hundred thousand head of cattle and perhaps double that number of small domestic beasts like sheep and goats. The soil over a great area of the park was not deep, water was scarce, and clearly the wild game was fighting a losing battle for survival. At first the Tanganyika Government's only reaction to the problem had been to resign itself to a compromise; it proposed to preserve two areas at either end of the park for the wild game and hand over all the central part, more than half the entire park, to the Masai.

At once there was an outcry from the wild life societies and by the time I reached Kenya a public and bitter controversy had arisen. Quite clearly a fundamental issue was involved: it was the ancient conflict between those· who believe that man has inviolable rights on earth – that all other forms of life are bound to succumb to his increasing needs – and those who quite simply disagree. And the issue was still further confused by the fact that the Masai, perhaps because of their very toughness and intransigence, are rather admired by white men in Africa in the same way as, too late, the Red Indian came to be admired in North America.

Then, however, the picture improved. In 1957 the Government of Tanganyika appointed a Committee of Inquiry to advise on the future of the Serengeti National Park. A number of eminent ecologists were called in to give their opinion; as a result, the Park has been enlarged in the western and central Serengeti area and is – to quote the Fauna Preservation Society – 'designed to ensure for the future the living space and migration routes of the famous herds of wild ungulates (hoofed animals) and their attendant predators ... a precious part of the world's inheritance.' The Ngorongoro crater has been excised from the Park and included in a Special Conservation Unit, and there is apparently some reason to hope – at least in the opinion of the experts – that the Masai and the wild-life will manage to coexist in peace. There have been other measures.

In Kenya the Governor, Sir Evelyn Baring, has issued a directive, the first of its kind, instructing all government officials to take a much stronger line over the preservation of wild game. In the Tsavo Park David Sheldrick appears to be getting the upper hand in his fight against the ivory poachers, and in Mombasa a new bonded warehouse has been set up for the ivory trade. This last is an important move. In the old days the traders bought their ivory on the open market and then took it back to their workshops around the town. It was no difficult thing for a dishonest trader to slip in quantities of poached tusks among those which had been legally bought. Under the new system each trader must have his workshop inside the bonded warehouse, where he will be under the eye of government inspectors.

More important perhaps than all this, there has been recently a sudden stirring of interest in the conservation of game among East African settlers everywhere. The new wild life societies in Kenya and Tanganyika are beginning to number some of the most influential people among their numbers. Even in the Rhodesias, where the wholesale slaughter of wild animals has been encouraged by the government year after year in the hope of stamping out the tsetse fly, new reserves and parks are being established.

Nothing can be done of course to restore the situation as it was, even twenty or thirty years ago; ninety per cent of African animals have been exterminated for ever. However, the chances of preserving the remaining ten per cent seem to be a little better than they were, and it may even be that the human instinct to kill all other living things on earth will wear itself out at last.

CHAPTER SIX

A MOST FORGIVING APE

JUST south of the equator, in the extreme south-western corner of Uganda, a chain of eight volcanoes rises to a height of 15,000 feet and straggles in a ragged line across the border into the Belgian Congo. This is one of the more grandiose spectacles in Central Africa, and it is in many ways a strange and disturbing place. Approaching it from the Uganda side you emerge quite suddenly on to the crest of a mountain pass, and there, all at once, the scene breaks out before you with the theatricality of a curtain lifted from a stage. Mount Muhavura, the first of the volcanoes, is a perfect cone with thick green jungle on its sides, and beyond this one glimpses the outlines of other, loftier peaks, usually with their tops neatly cut off by a bank of heavy cloud. The last two volcanoes on the Congo side are still active, and all the floor of the valley below them is dotted with black forbidding patches of lava. This is a region of landslides and earth tremors and nothing seems secure. Indeed, in recent years still another volcano has burst out of a stretch of level plain and has now risen to a height of six hundred feet.

For the most part the local African tribesmen live in a damp soporific heat around the lakes at the foot of the volcanoes, and they seldom go up into the cold jungles and the cloudy heights above; that area, the temperate and sub-alpine zone, has become the refuge of one of the rarest of all wild animals in Africa, the mountain gorilla.

The gorilla is something of a paradox in the African scene. One thinks one knows him very well. For a hundred years or more he has been killed, captured, and imprisoned in zoos. His bones have been mounted in natural history musuems everywhere, and he has always exerted a strong fascination upon scientists and romantics alike. He is the stereotyped monster of the horror films and the adventure books, and an obvious (though not perhaps strictly scientific) link with our ancestral past.

Yet the fact is we know very little about gorillas. No really satisfactory photograph has ever been taken of one in a wild state, no zoologist, however intrepid, has been able to keep the animal under close and constant observation in the dark jungles in which it lives. Carl Akeley, the American naturalist, led two expeditions to these volcanoes in the nineteen-twenties, and now lies buried here among the animals he loved so well. But even he was unable to discover how long the gorilla lives, or how or why it dies, nor was he able to define the exact social pattern of the family groups, or indicate the final extent of their intelligence. All this and many other things remain almost as much a mystery as they were when the French explorer Du Chaillu first described the animal to the civilized world a century ago. The Abominable Snowman who haunts the imagination of climbers in the Himalayas is hardly more elusive.

The little that is known about gorillas certainly makes you want to know a great deal more. Sir Julian Huxley has recorded that thrice in the London Zoo he saw an eighteen-month-old specimen trace the outline of its own shadow with its finger. 'No similar artistic initiative,' he writes, 'has been recorded for any other anthropoid, though we all know now that young chimpanzees will paint "pictures" if provided with the necessary materials.' Huxley speaks too of a traveller seeing a male gorilla help a female up a steep rock-step on Mount Muhavura, and gallantry of that kind is certainly not normal among animals. It is this 'human-ness' of the gorilla which is so beguiling. According to some observers he courts and makes love in the same way as humans do. Once the family is established it clings together. It feeds in a group in the thick bamboo jungles on the mountainside in the daytime, each animal making a tidy pile of its food – wild celery, bamboo shoots, and other leaves – and squatting down to eat it; and by night each member of the family makes its own bed by bending over and interlacing the bamboo fronds so as to form a kind of oval-shaped nest which is as comfortable and springy as a mattress. The father tends to make his bed just a foot or two from the ground, the mother a little higher, and the children (perhaps two or three of them) safely lodged in the branches up above.

When he walks (and usually a family will travel about half a mile a day), the gorilla takes the main weight on his short legs and rests lightly on the knuckles of his hands at the end of his very long arms. When he stands upright a full-grown male rises to six foot, but with that immense chest he is far heavier than any normal man could ever be. Six hundred pounds is not uncommon. His strength is incredible – certainly great enough to enable him to take a man in his hands and wrench his head off. The female is much smaller and lighter.

Miss J. H. Donisthorpe, who recently made a study of gorillas in the Muhavura area, says that the animals have a strong smell which she describes as a mixture of human sweat, manure, and charred wood. They have good eyesight but are probably deficient in both hearing and smelling. They appear to talk to one another, Miss Donisthorpe says, in high-pitched voices, not unlike that of a woman, or by smacking their lips or striking their cheeks, and the female, if alarmed, will scream. The male, on the other hand, is capable of making a frightening demonstration in the face of danger. He stays behind while his family gets away, rising to his feet and uttering a terrifying roar. Sometimes he will drum on his chest and shake the trees around him with every appearance of uncontrollable fury. In extremity he will charge.

But all this, Miss Donisthorpe assured us, is no more than shadow boxing as a general rule, for the gorilla is a gentle, kindly creature, a most forgiving ape who lives at peace with all the other animals, and his reputation for savagery and belligerence is nothing but a myth. When the animal charges the thing to do is to stand your ground and look him in the eye. Then he will turn aside and slip away through the undergrowth.

Nobody knows how many gorillas are left among the volcanoes or whether they are decreasing or increasing, but the numbers are very small, probably something between fifty and two hundred. Nowadays they are protected after a fashion and no one may legally shoot or capture them, but this still does not prevent the local tribesmen from killing them. If the gorillas spoil their crops (and the crops are being pushed steadily further up the mountainsides), or loot the honey from the wild beehives which the tribesmen have placed in the trees, then spearsmen track them to their lairs and take reprisals. Nine gorillas were butchered in this way just before I myself arrived in the area earlier this year.

It was, I must confess, only by chance that I found myself there at all, for I had been heading in a quite different direction from Tanganyika northwards to the valley of the upper Nile. I knew something about the gorilla sanctuary among the volcanoes, but had never planned to go there since the animals have grown very timid and difficult to get at, and few people ever manage to see them. It happened, however, that our safari (a modest one consisting of myself, a companion, and a Swahili boy all travelling together with our food and bedding in a single truck) had arrived at Kabale, the southernmost town in Uganda, and here we had decided to rest in comfortable surroundings for a couple of days.

Kabale is quite a landmark in central Africa. It possesses a delightful English inn set among lawns and terraced gardens. There is a well-kept golf-course just outside the grounds, and within the immediate neighbourhood of the hotel itself one can play tennis, badminton, croquet, bowls, table tennis, and possibly squash as well (though I never verified this). In the evening one drinks French wine at dinner, reads the magazines in the lounge, plays bridge, and listens to the radio. Very rightly the European inhabitants of East Africa take their holidays in this cool green place, for it bears a striking resemblance to any of the lusher golfing resorts in southern England, Sunningdale perhaps. It is not, however, the Africa that the traveller comes to see. Changing for dinner the night we arrived I remembered the gorillas. They lay only half a day's drive away through the mountains, and despite the heavy rain that had been falling the road, I discovered, was passable. Next morning we were on our way. It was not that we expected to see a gorilla any more than an amateur deep-sea fisherman will count on hooking a marlin or a sailfish at his first attempt; we were simply glad to be back in primitive Africa again and in an atmosphere where the unexpected might just possibly happen.

We came over the crest of the mountains and followed the sweep of the eagles far down into the valley below, to the little village of Kisoro at the foot of Muhavura and its neighbouring cone, Mount Mgahinga. Here one stays with the game warden, Mr M. W. Baumgartel, a man who, like Carl Akeley before him, devotes his life to the gorillas. Mr Baumgartel was not unoptimistic. If we rose early on the following morning, he said, he would give us guides to take us up the mountains. It would mean climbing to at least ten thousand feet and we would be walking all day, without any definite prospect of success; the very best we could hope for was one fleeting glimpse of a gorilla through the undergrowth.

Now I cannot, by any sort of indulgence, pretend that the climb we made on the following day was in any way exceptional. Many people have done it before and are still doing it. Miss Donisthorpe during her three months research on the gorillas used to make the ascent almost every day. I merely wish to record that for any middle-aged person of sedentary habits it is a considerable ordeal, and that only a sort of vanity or pig-headedness will keep him going: having once embarked on this enterprise he will feel no doubt, as I did, that he must keep on. A curious optimism intervenes; suddenly it becomes not only possible but imperative to clamber up every new height which would have seemed impossible at the outset of the journey. Having never given wild gorillas more than a passing thought in my life before, it now became absolutely essential that I should see one.

Our two guides turned out to be thin little Africans wearing battered suits and hats and anything less like mountaineers could hardly have been imagined. In point of fact, as we soon discovered, they were experts with hypersensitive powers of sight and smell and hearing. They were as indefatigable as the gorilla himself, and like all highly-trained trackers they appeared to feel their way through the bush as though they were moved by some sixth sense which attuned them to their quarry's instincts, so that they knew exactly which path to follow and where to stop and change direction. Certainly it would have been impossible to find the gorillas without them.

We drove first to the foot of the mountains, and then with one guide in front and the other behind we set off on foot along an uncompromising track that led directly upwards to the saddle between Muhavura and Mghinga. A watercourse rushed down the mountain beside us, a bright hot sun burst through the clouds, and as we climbed the valley behind us spread out marvellously below; beyond it range after range of hills rolled away towards the Congo. But after the first few minutes I gave up looking at any of these splendid things. Instead I kept my head resolutely downwards, concentrating upon the next step ahead. It seemed at times that we were climbing almost perpendicularly. Pretty soon we were in the bamboo belt. Bamboo grows on these central African mountains in thin stalks from ten to twenty feet high, and so thickly that it is often impenetrable. One of the guides took his panga, a broad hooked blade about eighteen inches long, and cut me a walking-stick. I suppose it helped, but already I was getting beyond caring.

Then at last after some two hours or more we came out on a clearing and rested. We were now just below 8,000 feet, and all around us unexpected things were growing, banks of huge nettles, orchids sprouting from the grass, plants like bullrushes, and those bright flame-coloured flowering reeds which as children we used to call red-hot pokers. The bamboo here had thinned out a little, and on the heights of the two mountains above we could see the curious productions of the alpine zones, giant heather, giant groundsel, and giant lobelias. Everything here was giant size but reduced to the appearance of littleness by the tremendous space around us. A vast cloud, shot through with sunlight, was tearing off the crest of Muhavura.

I remembered Baumgartel telling me that at this height elephants, leopards, and hyenas roamed about as well as the gorilla, but I could see no sign of movement anywhere along the mountain slopes, and in the sky only the long circular sweeps of the eagles sailing by. The silence seemed absolute.

Presently, when my companion and I had gathered our breath a little, the guides indicated that we must go on again. This, for me, had I only known it, was where the impossible began. Hitherto we had at least proceeded on our feet in an upright position. Now we headed into a thick scrub of mingled bamboo and hypericum trees and often the only possible method of getting ahead was on all fours like a gorilla. The guides would not at this stage cut a path with their pangas lest the noise should alarm the animals, and so it was necessary to haul oneself bodily through the undergrowth, and always we kept going upward.

By midday we had passed the ten thousand foot mark, but I am not really able to recall the incidents of these hours, for red lights had long since begun to dance in front of my eyes and however quickly I gasped for breath it never seemed possible to get enough air into my lungs. The guides kept casting about in different directions and disappearing into the scrub, but then they would call to one another with an insistent bell-like whistle and that was the only sound I heard except for the noise created by my own beastly wallowing in the thickets. We seemed to be following some sort of a trail, since I saw gorilla droppings on the ground at intervals, and finally we came up with a group of their nests. There they all were, the big ones and the little ones, exactly as they had been described. I had an impulse to climb up and try one of those springy beds, but that would have meant using up more energy when I had none to spare, and anyway the nests were fouled with droppings. I stared dully at a little pile of shavings on the ground; obviously a gorilla had sat here peeling the bark off a twig before he ate it, and I looked at one of the guides interrogatively. But he shook his head. This was an old nesting place and the gorilla family had long since moved on. We started our crawling climb again.

Once or twice, I recall, I experienced a moment of fear and it was fear bordering on panic. What on earth was there to protect us if a gorilla suddenly appeared out of the bushes only a yard or two away? We had no rifle. It would be quite impossible to run away in this scrub. I did not now for one instant believe all the stories about how the gorilla was always more frightened of human beings than they were of him. Here was I in the jungle, a human being, or at any rate what was left of one, and I knew, with that certainty that only a profound searching of the heart can reveal, that I was more frightened than any gorilla could ever be. There was no question whatever of my standing my ground and looking him firmly in the eye. I was going to stiffen into paralysis with my eyes tightly shut and wait for my head to be torn off.

But then fatigue created a kind of mental anaesthetic. We had been climbing now for more than four hours and were evidently getting nowhere. Suddenly it became more important to stop and lie down than to see a gorilla, and fear was overwhelmed by the sheer physical pain in my chest and legs. Let the others go on and see all the gorillas they wanted. I was going to stop here and now. As I subsided on to a patch of open ground I called to the others and waved them on. A little surprisingly, I felt, they did go on and left me alone. But then what did it matter? Let all the gorillas in the world come and get me: I really did not care.

The next ten minutes were as timeless as only the amnesia of utter exhaustion could make them, and it seemed that I had been resting there in a daze for an hour at least when I opened my eyes and saw my companions standing above me excitedly urging me to get up. They had come on a fresh gorilla track at last, an entire family on the move just ahead of us. And indeed as we scrambled on again I saw fresh droppings on the ground and broken branches that clearly had only recently been wrenched from the trees. But it was no good. After twenty minutes my legs had turned to water again and against the evident displeasure of the guides I demanded lunch.

In the earlier part of our journey through Africa my friend and I had always chosen a pleasant place with a view or beside some stream in which to eat our lunch. Here, however, we sank down on to the earth where we were and dully stuffed the food into our mouths. There was no view anywhere, nothing but the oppressive and silent scrub. The two guides watched us impatiently, squatting a yard or two away. Yet it was amazing what those hunks of bread and meat did: life and hope began to flow through the blood again, and a cup of sweet coffee from a thermos flask accelerated the process. I rose groggily to my feet and faced the impossible once more. We fell into line again with myself drawing up in the rear.

The guides now adjured us to keep the strictest silence, and in fact it was this silence that dominated all the last moments of our climb. It closed around one with a thick palpable druglike heaviness, almost as if one's ears were stuffed with cotton wool or one's sense of hearing had suddenly failed; layer on layer of silence. And this void, this nothingness of sound, was suddenly torn apart by a single high-pitched bellowing scream. It was bizarre to the point of nightmare. It was as if one had received a sudden unexpected blow on the back of the head. As I stood there, heart thumping, transfixed with shock, one of the guides grabbed me by the arm and half dragged and half pushed me through the undergrowth towards a little rise where the others were standing. I looked at the point where they were staring and

I remember calling out aloud, 'Oh my God, how wonderful!'

And the truth is he was wonderful. He was a huge shining male, half crouching, half standing, his mighty arms akimbo. I had not been prepared for the blackness of him; he was a great craggy pillar of gleaming blackness, black crew-cut hair on his head, black deep-sunken eyes towards us, huge rubbery black nostrils, and a black beard. He shifted his posture a little, still glaring fixedly upon us, and he had the dignity and majesty of prophets. He was the most distinguished and splendid animal I ever saw and I had only one desire at that moment: to go forward towards him, to meet him and to know him: to communicate. This experience (and I am by no means the only one to feel it in the presence of a gorilla) is utterly at variance with one's reactions to all other large wild animals in Africa. If the lion roars, if you get too close to an elephant and he fans out his ears, if the rhinoceros lowers his head and turns in your direction, you have, if you are unarmed and even sometimes if you are, just one impulse and that is to run away. The beast you feel is savage, intrinsically hostile, basically a murderer. But with the gorilla there is an instant sense of recognition. You might be badly frightened, but in the end you feel you will be able to make some gesture, utter some sound, that the animal will recognize and understand. At all events you do not have the same instinct to turn and bolt.

Afterwards I remembered another thing. Normally, when you come up against a rare wild animal in Africa, you grab your binoculars or your camera at once. It is a simple reflex action. This gorilla was thirty yards away and divided from us by tangled undergrowth and might not perhaps have made a very good photograph, but we could certainly have seen him more clearly through glasses. Yet none of us moved. In my own case (and I suspect in the case of my friend as well) I felt that there was not a second to be lost of this contact, not even the few instants required to put the binoculars to my eyes. I wanted to see him naturally and I wanted to see him whole.

And now abruptly he rose to his full height. Had I really been about to give expression to my sub-conscious desire to move towards him I expect that, at this moment, I would have paused, for he was tremendous in his great height and strength. It was a question now as to whether or not he would beat on his chest and charge, so as to give his family (unseen by us but certainly lurking somewhere there in the bush) further time to get away, but, in fact, he did neither of these things. He lifted his head and gave vent to another of those outlandish and terrifying barking-screams. Once again it seemed to bring every living thing in the bush, including one's own heart, to a full stop. Then he dropped on to his hands and melted away. There was, of course, no chance of following him; despite his size he could travel many times faster than we could.

That was the end of the show, and it had lasted I suppose a couple of hundred seconds. Yet still, after much wandering through Africa in the last few years, I rate this as the most exciting encounter that has come my way; and I remember how, no longer any need for silence, the guides with their pangas slashed a path for us to return through the bush, and how they grinned and were pleased because we were pleased, and how I went down the mountain like a young gazelle in two hours straight, never a touch of fatigue, never a thought for my blistered feet after such a happy day.

CHAPTER SEVEN

THE KARAMOJONG

BETWEEN the Equator and 5 degrees north in East Africa there is an area round Lake Rudolf which though technically a part of Kenya and Uganda is in reality a quite separate country, an island, as it were, inside the vast land mass of this corner of the continent, just as you might say that Switzerland is an island inside Europe. The real frontiers are racial and geographical, not political. To the north lie the Abyssinian mountains, to the east the Indian Ocean, to the south the White Highlands of Kenya, and in the west the Nile flows by along the borders of the Belgian Congo.

In the normal way few people visit this area, since a good deal of it is desert, or at all events semi-desert, and the British in any case don't encourage casual travellers. In recent years the Abyssinian tribes have been raiding down from the north in search of cattle, and an intermittent frontier warfare goes on. Few of the skirmishes amount to anything really serious, but in the last twelve months or so about two hundred Africans have been killed. Quite apart from this very few roads or tracks exist, and travellers are advised to take two vehicles with them in case of a breakdown in some unfrequented spot.

There is another reason for the isolation of this region. The local tribesmen – people like the Karamojong and the Turkana – have not taken to western civilization in the way nearly all other Africans are doing. They are not hostile to it – they accept with quite good grace the rules and the laws laid down by the British district commissioners – but they see no point in wearing European clothes, in using money, or in working long hours in the hot sun when there is no real necessity for doing so. The Karamojong is a warrior and a herdsman of cattle, and he wants to live his own life. In the main the British have accepted this state of affairs, and the result has been that here, and almost only here, can you stand aside from the suburbanization of East Africa : the shops, petrol stations, schools, factories, and westernized farms which have spread over so much of the country in the last twenty years.

I had wanted to make a journey through this area ever since the day, early in 1957, when Rennie Bere, the Director of the Game Parks in Uganda, wrote to me saying that he was seriously disturbed about what was happening to the wild animals there. It seemed that the tribesmen were not only killing one another but were demolishing the game as well, and they were doing it by the particularly brutal method known as the fire ring. This is a simple device by which the shrubs and dry grass are set on fire around the herds of grazing animals which are then driven into the flames. Giraffe and even elephant are comparatively easy to kill once they become bewildered and terrified by the smoke and heat, especially when the tribesmen, running like greyhounds, hurl their spears from many directions at once.

Bere spoke particularly of the Karamoja district – the home of the Karamojong – a stretch of land some ten thousand square miles in extent that runs up to the Sudanese border in the extreme north-eastern corner of Uganda. It was the border tribes, he said, who were doing most of the damage along the Kidepo River there.

Finally in 1958 I planned the journey. It was to take me first up to Karamoja and then east across the Kenya border to the Turkana country on the western shores of Lake Rudolf. The third and last leg of the trip was to be another excursion which I had been promising myself for a long time past : a journey down the Nile from its source on the Equator in Lake Victoria to Khartoum, a couple of thousand miles away in the centre of the Sudan.

To get to my first objective, Karamoja, I was more or less bound to start from Entebbe, the capital of Uganda on Lake Victoria, and my wife and I flew down there from our home in Italy one night in February. The pleasant shock of that sudden translation from Europe to Central Africa never fails. In Italy we had been having a foul winter, a combination of icy rain and the flu, *La Asiatica*. But now in Entebbe in the early morning, divided from the Roman rain by one short night, we were enfolded by a heavy steady warmth and the scent of tropical flowers. A bird which is called the green cuckoo uttered its maniac cry, a noise which is like a shout of insane laughter, and we ate iced pawpaw on a veranda overlooking the lake. Twenty-four hours later we had made our safari arrangements – everything seems to be called a safari in central Africa these days – and were on our way. Our route lay eastward along the north shore of Lake Victoria, and then northward to Moroto, the capital of Karamoja, a distance of about 300 miles.

For this first stage of our journey we were keeping to the beaten track, and we travelled with just one truck and the usual paraphernalia of mosquito-nets, canned food, and water bags. The cook-driver-interpreter we had engaged was a man named Juma, and he had travelled widely through Africa as a soldier in the King's African Rifles; but we were pleased to hear that he had never been to Karamoja. He spoke of the Karamojong with a rolling of his eyes and a distasteful expression on his face, calling them 'very savage, very wild'. This is something you have to get used to in Africa now : the rich relation attitude, the half-embarrassed, half-contemptuous manner with which the westernized African refers to the naked tribesmen in the village. And in fact there is a fantastic contrast between these lush provinces on Lake Victoria and the wilderness to the north. Here in a damp, soporific breeze you are surrounded by groves of coffee, pawpaws, pineapples, sugar-cane, and bananas. Most of these exotic plants are no more indigenous to Africa than the petrol stations, but they thrive here with an artificial hot-house exuberance. The metalled road runs through land that was an unexplored jungle only a few decades ago, and now might be anywhere in Florida.

This sudden uneven bound from the Stone Age into the mid twentieth century has left some queer anachronisms in its wake, and at times one has an uneasy feeling that something has gone wrong in the process, too many threads have been broken, too many experiments left uncompleted. At the town of Jinja, for example, there used to be a waterfall – the Ripon Falls – as recently as 1954, and a plaque beside it announced that here in 1862 Captain John Speke discovered the source of the Nile. Now both plaque and waterfall are submerged beneath the waters of a hydro-electric dam.

Below the dam, where the river begins its four thousand mile course to the Mediterranean, you are quite likely to see, as we did, a fisherman with barbaric tribal scars on his face. He stands in a boat made out of a hollowed tree trunk and casts a green nylon Japanese net into the stream. Next year he will have an outboard motor-boat, and already the first frogman with an aqualung has plunged into the lake among the hippopotami and crocodiles. The circular African huts you see on the lake shore remain the traditional size and shape, but now they are made of prefabricated aluminium instead of grass, and they are dry, practical, and hideous.

It is the same thing too further down the Nile, where it joins Lake Albert on the Congo border. I have described how on an earlier visit to Uganda it was quite a common thing for the women to wear nothing but a couple of bunches of fresh leaves which were tied to a string around their waists, and a very pretty sight it was. But things are already changing. Nowadays even the youngest girls wear a one-piece garment that looks like a loose-cover for an armchair and is called a Mother Hubbard. Later on during this present trip, however, I noticed that many of these girls seemed to bulge and rustle somewhat as they walked, and when I inquired about this I was told that they still go out and gather the fresh leaves every morning. But now they wear them underneath the Mother Hubbard. Just occasionally, when some celebration is taking place and banana wine has been brewed, the Mother Hubbard is taken off, and then they dance with a rhythmical stamping of their bare feet on the ground precisely as they always did before the missionaries arrived and the new cotton ginnery was established on the hill. But I would guess that all this too will have stopped within a year or two, and then, decorously, in cotton frocks, stockings, and leather shoes, they will gather in some concrete shack to dance a samba or a rhumba which they will regard as the latest and smartest thing from America, and never recognize (and perhaps would be dismayed to recognize) a rhythm that had its origins here in Africa.

Then there are the English inns. Several of them dot the route we are taking, and they have a special Edwardian charm with African overtones. In the warm evening, that best moment of the African day, one drives up to a rambling verandaed building, and in the courtyard where you park the car flowering jacarandas, flamboyants, and tropical poinsettias sprout up past the bedroom windows. The branches sing with myriads of brightly-coloured birds. Inside the building the atmosphere is that of an English country pub of thirty or forty years ago. There stands the billiard table, its cloth getting a little rusty now and not all the cues are straight. In the lounge (cane chairs, chintz curtains, and hat-racks with dim oval mirrors) bound copies of the London *Daily Sketch* and the *Illustrated London News* lie about. The bar is a rather furtive sanctuary down the passage, and is placarded with such announcements as: 'No Credit', 'No Dogs', and perhaps an appeal for the vicar's Christmas fund. Then too, among the sporting prints and the whisky advertisements there is likely to be a series of coloured caricatures that takes you back to the early days of the British in Africa. There are the whiskered faces of the empire builders, the district commissioners, the policemen, and the engineers, who once habitually came in here for their evening 'sundowners' of beer or whisky. Their ghosts have not quite departed yet. In the bedrooms upstairs the 'boy' (white-turbaned, bare-footed, and aged perhaps thirty-five or forty) still brings you your morning cup of tea and prepares the evening tub.

One feels that all this has come and gone – or at any rate is going – a little too precipitately and completely, leaving hardly a trace behind. The new hotel on the airfield down the road is frequented by a new race of men, travelling salesmen, and officials with briefcases, and it overlays the Edwardian past with a certain ruthlessness, a kind of ready-made banality. The English language itself is becoming contorted into a curious sort of lingua franca that bears less and less resemblance to the mother tongue, much in the same way as Swahili has confounded the original Arabic. Africans struggle over words learned in a chance half-hour at school, and arrive at their own scheme of pronunciation, sometimes with comic effects. Juma came running in to my wife one day saying: 'Memsahib, where's your camera? There's an historic outside.' We looked at him blankly, but he kept on repeating excitedly, 'an historic, an historic,' and it was not until we glanced outside and saw an ostrich pacing by that we discovered what he meant.

Then for some reason I recall an Indian youth walking up a village street one evening, and he called to his companions who were standing outside a tailor's shop, 'I'm willing for pictures. Who's willing for pictures?' They were all willing, and with a gentle murmuring of singsong Indian voices went off together to the movie which was being shown in an iron shanty at the end of the street.

It was no accident, incidentally, that they should have met at a tailor's shop, for there are at least two or three of them even in the smallest villages. From dawn until nightfall men (never women) sit pedalling away at sewing machines on the pavement making clothes for the inhabitants – sometimes the first clothes they have ever worn.

All this, we found, altered in an instant on the following day when we turned north and crossed the border into Karamoja. Lake Victoria is nearly four thousand feet above sea level, but now we dropped down into a wide flat land-

scape dotted with stark rocky hills and the metalled road
soon dwindled into a sand track. There was a hot dry wind
with a whiff of the desert in it, and little by little all signs
of cultivation fell away. Half a dozen giraffe browsed
round us while we ate lunch under a group of thorn trees,
the only shade for miles around, and then we continued on
over dusty plains all through the afternoon until we reached
Moroto in the evening.

Moroto, the official headquarters of Karamoja district, is
a delightful place, the last island of normal civilization
before you push on to the north. Apart from the African
village there cannot be more than twenty or thirty buildings in the township, but these are dotted about among
gardens and green lawns, and a ten-thousand-foot mountain covered with scrub and jungle rises behind the settle-
ment. Already here you are in the midst of the country
occupied by the Karamojong tribe, and we spent the next
three days among them.

I had been doing some reading about these people before
leaving Italy, so I knew more or less what to expect; even
so this first meeting was something of a shock. The men
were all about six-foot tall, and they had the slim hipless
figures of long-distance runners which in fact they were.
They walked about with a sort of stately assurance, not
exactly parading their nakedness, but obviously conscious
of their own beauty. They were quite friendly, they never
failed to wave to us and call out *Jambo*, the universal word
of greeting in this part of Africa, but there was a slight air
of condescension in the way they did it. Simple though it
is, the Karamojong's toilette must take up a good deal of
time, for it involves an elaborate shaving and plaiting of the
hair, and upon their heads they wear a close-fitting little
hat such as you might see women wearing at a cocktail
party, except that in this case the hat is of human hair
matted together with clay. Often it has a couple of short
ostrich feathers stuck jauntily on top. Around the neck
goes a tight necklace of coloured beads, often with armlets
and bangles round their arms to match. I saw no ear-rings,

but many of the men had a bone button about the size of a silver dollar attached to a hole made in the lower lip. The belts around their waists were also articles of pure adornment, for they supported nothing whatever. Most of these belts were made of a silver-coloured wire and it stood out brightly against the deep black skin. (One man I heard of had somehow acquired a Boy Scout's belt with 'Be Prepared' on the buckle, but that was exceptional and an anti-climax.) Occasionally a short rust-coloured cloak is thrown over one shoulder, and every man carries a small two-or-three-legged wooden stool which serves both as a seat and a pillow, and which from a distance looks like a woman's handbag (the ground in these arid districts is excessively hard and prickly to sit down on). In brief, the Karamojong warrior wears the kinds of accessories a well-dressed western woman might have, but without the clothes.

It would be a mistake, however, to regard him as effeminate, for his preferred diet, like that of the Masai, is a mixture of fresh milk and blood, and he always carries at least one spear as tall as himself, beautifully balanced and with a blade so sharp it is often protected with a leather sheath. Except for minding his cattle the warrior does no work, he carries no burdens and builds nothing; it is his business to preserve himself for the day when he must kill, or at any rate draw the blood of some living thing, whether animal or human, with the tip of his spear. This proves his virility and makes him a desirable partner in a marriage. He notches up his score of victims on his own body by making little cicatrices on his skin, and each of these scars has a meaning. For example, a line of them on the right breast means that he has killed a man, a line on the left breast a woman.

This killing, of course, is not an everyday thing, and the British act drastically with an outright murderer if they can manage to catch him. Yet murder does occur, and fairly frequently; and this we soon discovered for ourselves. We were driving one day along a particularly deserted track when suddenly a group of tribesmen appeared out of the bushes before us. One of them was a policeman, an askari, dressed in the khaki shorts and tunic provided by the British. The rest were naked, and they held up their spears to bring our vehicle to a stop – and stop we did, at once. They seemed very excited and nervous and it was some time before Juma, speaking Swahili, managed to discover that a man had been speared to death in a village close beside the track during the night – the body was still lying out there in the sun. A runner had been sent off with this news to the nearest British police post twenty miles away. The askari wanted to know if we would pick up this man and take him on his way, because he feared that fighting might break out in the village at any moment, and help was wanted quickly.

We caught up with the runner round the next bend and he was a splendid figure, loping smoothly along at a steady five miles an hour, his spear and his stool in one hand and in the other a cleft stick in which was fixed a message written on a slip of white paper. I judged from his grizzled grey beard that the man must have been about forty years of age, but he had on his face an expression of extreme alarm, even of panic. He was like a child who has been asked to do something too difficult and he clutched his cleft stick as though it were made of fragile porcelain, holding it rigidly upright in his left hand. He clambered into the back of the truck and out of sheer awkwardness and nervousness rested the tip of his spear about an inch from my wife's neck. And thus, a little uneasily, we bumped along to the police post and handed him over to the sergeant.

Back in Moroto I asked about these killings and was told that they are nearly always concerned with cattle, and, after cattle, women. According to the late Professor C. G. Seligman, an authority on the subject, it is impossible to exaggerate the importance of cattle to these tribes. Cattle, he says, 'are so important that if an adjective stands by itself the noun it qualifies is always understood to be "cow" '. Like the Masai, the Karamojong adores his cattle. He caresses them, sings to them in the fields, drinks their milk and blood (which he takes from a vein in the neck), and uses them as currency for bargaining. Cattle are almost his entire wealth, and the more of them he has the better. The British have recently managed to stamp out rinderpest, the main cattle disease, and the herds now roam in such numbers that the land is turning into dust. But still the tribes, driven by an overpowering instinct, feel impelled to go on breeding more stock, even though the more intelligent chiefs are perfectly well aware that drought and famine are bound to overtake them in the end.

Naturally there has been a wild inflation in the use of cattle as currency. In order to buy a wife now a man must pay the girl's father as much as sixty head. In our civilization this might be the equivalent of finding something like fifteen hundred pounds, or even more, and so in some places the poorer young men have resorted to time payment; they produce ten cattle this year and another ten next year, and so they go on until the girl is paid off. Then they set to work buying a second wife. This is where the killing comes in. It happens from time to time that a man will become impatient for a wife, and he then goes out by night on cattle raids. These raids are carried out with marvellous endurance and skill – a practised man can drive a mob of cattle thirty miles before the morning breaks – but sometimes the owners catch up with the marauders and then the spears fly through the air. Raids and counter-raids were going on in the Karamoja the whole time we were there, and in the prison in Moroto there were quite a number of prisoners who were doing long stretches for cattle theft. They did not seem to mind particularly. Two years or ten, it was all the same to them, since they had no sense of time, and meanwhile they were eating well.

To the western mind it is something of a mystery that the Karamojong should value his wife so highly that he is willing to commit theft and murder for her, for by no excess of chivalry can she be called a beautiful object. Compared to her peacock mate she is dowdier than a peahen. She is short, scrawny, and physically dirty. For a short moment around her fifteenth year her body may achieve a certain grace and firmness, but that brief springtime is soon gone and by the time she is twenty she is older than the rocks on which she sits (she is allowed of course no stool). She shaves half her skull and twists the remaining hair into strands that look like a greasy mop. She loads her ears and neck with a mass of coiled wire (never removed) which must weigh a good ten pounds or more. Still more wire is bound around her short arms and legs and she ties a ragged goat's skin round her waist. Arms, face, and midriff are decorated with a pattern of tribal tattoos, and the whole ensemble is topped off with an unwashed shawl or an old sack thrown over the shoulders.

I was given two explanations of the fascination exerted by the Karamojong woman, the first of which seems sound enough. She represents wealth almost as much as the cattle do. She does the work, the drawing of water, the building of huts, even digging in the fields; and she produces the children. The second explanation is more doubtful. According to this, physical beauty in a woman plays no part at all in marriage; in fact, it is avoided. The Karamojong male proceeds on the presumption that a beautiful woman will be desired by all men and that consequently she herself will want all men. And so as a wife she is more trouble than she is worth.

Whether all this be true or not, the fact remains that most of the women we saw were by no means crushed by work and child-bearing. I used to watch them gathering round the waterholes in the morning. They were very gay, and they chattered incessantly even in the midday heat when the men were spreadeagled asleep in the shade under the acacia trees or simply squatting silently on their stools, secure in their beauty and in their power, for long hours at a stretch, of thinking of absolutely nothing.

Dr Samuel Johnson has said somewhere that 'all the importunities and perplexities of business are softness and luxury compared with the incessant cravings of vacancy and the unsatisfactory expedients of idleness'. This simply does not apply to the Karamojong. In their obvious pleasure in suspended animation, in sheer vacancy of mind, they can be compared only to the basking crocodile. This is not decadence nor is it torpor. It is virility in extreme repose. There are times, notably when a cattle raid is on or at the approach of a new moon, when the somnolent villages wake up. The Karamojong have no drums, but on these occasions they drink deeply of a strong beer made of maize, and then, rousing up their bedraggled mates, they dance the whole night through.

These sudden changes, these rapid shifts from primitive action to an almost lethean calm, create an atmosphere which seemed to me to be much more stimulating than that of the comfortable half-westernized world we had left behind on Lake Victoria. Here, at least, on these hot plains (most of Karamoja is only three thousand feet above the sea), we knew exactly where we were; we were back in the stone age. And we found it both releasing and exciting.

So too, apparently, did the white men who were administering the district. We used to meet them at the government rest-house at Moroto (there are no hotels at all in Karamoja) when they came in from the outlying districts to replenish stores and collect their mail. Nowhere in Africa, or indeed hardly anywhere else for that matter, have I met people so interested in their work. It filled their lives. Most of these men were young, unmarried, and paid on a scale which would shock a good cook or a head-waiter in a restaurant. Some of them lived in camps without electricity or running water, and often for days or even weeks on end never saw another white man. They knew that their jobs were unlikely to continue; even the most optimistic of them did not think the British would remain in Uganda for another fifteen years. Yet none of this appeared to cloud their enthusiasm. They were absorbed in the practical business of building new roads and bridges, of damming back the rivers and experimenting with soils and crops; and not unnaturally the local disputes among the tribes were of much more interest to them than all the summit conferences and the remote politics of the outside world. Karamoja is regarded as a tough and lonely district, and it is the practice of the British colonial service to move officials around every few years so that all have a spell in the more favoured places along Lake Victoria and the Nile. Yet most of these men had volunteered for a second term in Karamoja, and some were hoping to continue for a third. Not many took a moralistic attitude about what they were doing; they were quite simply enjoying themselves, or at all events they were too occupied to feel that sense of uncertainty and rootlessness that sometimes overtakes white men in the more politically developed parts of Africa. I noticed that the books they read tended to deal with technical subjects and were of the do-it-yourself kind; books on bridge-building, animal husbandry, medicine, fishing, and photography.

One other thing was apparent. They did not dislike the local Africans – they rather admired them – and as far as I could make out the Karamojong had no animosity towards white men. Perhaps this is a feudal and therefore temporary relationship, but at least it is a refreshing change from the tense colour-politics that bedevil the scene elsewhere in Africa. The simple rule seems to be that the more primitive an area is, the better whites and blacks get on together. Even the most rabid nationalist would have difficulty in proving that the Karamojong are being exploited. No white man is permitted to own land in their district (or in the rest of Uganda either). Taxes are trifling and such services as medical attention for both men and cattle are provided free. Money comes into Karamoja rather than goes out. Nor could it be said that there is any sweated or underpaid labour in the area, since the tribesmen quite definitely prefer not to work at all if they can help it.

But probably in the end it is the quality of plain uncluttered space which is the most satisfactory thing about living in these parts, and this we discovered when we finally moved off northwards again towards our ultimate objective, the Kidepo River. Moroto itself was remote enough, but now the empty plain expanded before us and quivered in a mirage under the hills. Giant cacti and acacia trees sprouted out of the dry earth. We had the sensation of really heading into the blue, and every bend in the track was the beginning of a fresh discovery.

All this corner of north-eastern Uganda was by-passed by the early explorers, and it was left to a more footloose character named Bell to open up the country to white men. In African legend Karamoja Bell is a kind of Buffalo Bill. He is the most famous of all elephant hunters, and the havoc he created was tremendous. He first arrived on the East African coast at Mombasa in 1897, as a young man of twenty, and was employed for a time as a lion-killer on the Kenya-Uganda railway. Then, after a spell as a goldminer in the Yukon, and a soldier in the Boer War, he came back to Mombasa and headed inland for the unknown wastes of Karamoja. Charles Darwin once estimated that in 900 years two elephants can become a million, and if any proof were needed for that statement Bell found it here. He came on vast herds that were beyond an ivory-hunter's dream, countless thousands of animals that had been browsing, unmolested, across these plains since immemorial time; and he spent the next twenty-five years blowing them out of existence. In his book *The Wanderings of an Elephant Hunter* Bell speaks of shooting twenty big bulls in a single day, and there is no reason to doubt this, for there are many people in East Africa who still remember his safaris returning to the coast, scores of porters each carrying a tusk on his shoulder. Taking each tusk as weighing forty pounds, and they must certainly have been as heavy as that, a single day's bag of twenty bulls would represent about £1,200 worth of ivory at present market prices.

Karamoja Bell had the genuine hunter's obsession for the beasts he killed, and a certain poetry of feeling about them – he speaks of their 'quiet, persistent flitting away' into the bush – and one must admire his courage. Yet it is a little sad now to drive across these plains and find that hardly an animal has been left behind. It looks the sort of place where at least the zebra ought to run. But nothing moves.

It was late in the afternoon when we approached the border of the Sudan, and then, having camped for the night, we drove on to a place called Opotipot the following day. Now at last we were in the country Rennie Bere had spoken of in his letter about the fire rings and the raiding tribesmen. It was as grand a landscape as anything in central Africa. Great green hills and towers of black rock thrust up out of the river valleys, and there was utter silence everywhere. This was a region infested by the tsetse fly, and in recent years a swathe has been cleared through the trees in which the fly breeds so as to make a barrier against the spread of the plague into Uganda. But even that huge unnatural gash in the forest could not quite destroy the freshness and mysteriousness which seems to pervade any African scene that has been left untouched through the centuries.

The camp at Opotipot consisted of a few thatched huts on a hilltop, and except that it served as a base for the Game Ranger on his visits to the area, there was no other reason for its existence. The thing I remember about this place is its permanent primordial stillness. One noted, with a traveller's satisfaction, that one was at a sort of crossroads here, that the mountains spread away in one direction to Abyssinia, in another to the Sudan, in another to Kenya, and in another back into Uganda. But none of these place-names counted for very much, nothing marked these frontiers, and certainly none of the tribesmen took much notice of them. It was a wilderness with no defined edges, and it quietly went its own way. There is an odd strength to be found in such remoteness, in knowing that no one very quickly can come to your assistance if things go wrong.

A group of African game scouts were living at the camp, and soon after we arrived one of them came to us with the news that the head-man, the sergeant, was ill. It did not seem to be serious and I sent him some aspirin. But then later in the day the messenger came back and said that now the corporal was stricken as well, and both of them were very bad. I went down to their hut and found the two men lying on the ground, limp and exhausted. They complained of pains in the stomach, and they could tell me nothing except that that morning they had eaten beans. The eating of half-cooked green beans which subsequently swell up in the stomach is the cause of one of the older and simpler illnesses among the Africans, but I knew nothing of this at the time. I went through the gesture of prodding the two men in the place where, vaguely, I imagined their appendices to be. Africans are wonderful patients. Hospital nurses will tell you that they behave much better than white men; they do not become demoralized, and with childish implicit trust will faithfully do the things that they are told to do. Yet at the same time they can be possessed with a fatalistic despair, a superstitious belief that some evil spirit has singled them out for destruction and that it is useless to resist. Africa is full of stories of how perfectly healthy men will decline and die simply because they have been placed under some tribal taboo. But you never know how far this superstition works. I had heard of one recent case where a young girl who was about to have a baby was brought into hospital paralysed almost up to the neck with poliomyelitis. When they undressed her they found her shoulders covered with fresh scars, and these she explained had been made by a witch doctor to whom she had gone for preliminary treatment. Once in the hospital, however, she was prepared to accept the white man's magic, and she followed the doctor's instructions with such strength of mind that she soon regained the use of her arms. The baby was born and was quite healthy.

So now, remembering these things confusedly, I looked down at my two patients who were slowly turning green about the lips, and it seemed inconceivable that two such huge powerful men could have been laid low so suddenly, and equally inconceivable that they would ever get well again. Indeed, it was confidently accepted in the camp that they would die. I found in my kit a bottle of Alka-Seltzer tablets (which I discovered later was emphatically NOT the right medicine) and dropped a couple of them into a mug of rather muddy brackish water which was all we had available at the time. (Opotipot means mud-hole.) The patients rose on their elbows and watched the fizzing with an intense hypnotized interest. They then drank up the mixture with such evident faith that I myself began to think that there must be some magic in the stuff; and I repeated the dose through the night. These additional draughts of liquid can only have made the green beans expand still further and have caused the two men more pain. But they had recovered by the morning, and although they did not thank me (thanks are regarded as an unnecessary ceremony among the tribesmen), there was a friendly and confident air about the camp, and I began to understand how it was that so many European officials like to go off and live alone with these people in their distant villages.

It was a queer party that assembled at Opotipot during the next few days; John Blower, the Karamoja game ranger, arrived in a two-seater plane (there was a level stretch of land in a nearby valley), and he was piloted by Dr William Longhurst, a zoologist of the University of California. Like ourselves, they had come to look at the wild animals along the border. Then there was the local tsetse control officer, a squat and heavily-bearded man with a nautical air that reminded one somehow of the sailors in Gilbert and Sullivan's *H.M.S. Pinafore*. He dropped in from his camp some twenty miles away, and he was soon followed by a British District Commissioner who was chasing a wounded elephant and happened to be passing by. Gun bearers, askaris, game scouts, and Karamojong porters completed the cast.

If there was no actual drama among us there was at least a certain eccentricity in our comings and goings during the next few days. The District Commissioner was in a somewhat harassed state. He had shot his elephant five days before, a young bull with 50-lb. tusks, and he could not forgive himself for having missed the vital spot with his shot, the small path into the brain in the centre of the skull, even though the animal was moving fast towards him at the time and was in the midst of the herd. It had been wounded in the body. In normal circumstances the tracking down of a wounded elephant is an arduous business, but not too difficult for an experienced man. Here in the north of Karamoja, however, there was no paraphernalia of hunting cars and of comfortable well-equipped camps to return to at night. It is one of the very few places in Africa where you still proceed on foot. The District Commissioner, in fact, was hunting precisely as Karamoja Bell had hunted fifty years ago; that is to say, he had set off into the wilds with a line of twenty porters following behind, each with a load on his head. Equipment had been cut down to the essentials; he slept out in the open at night, and made do with the most primitive meals (it is the usual thing on these foot-safaris to take a few live goats along with you, and these are butchered and eaten day by day as you go along), and except for the porters he was alone. These arrangements, because of their quietness and simplicity, can provide joys which the ordinary tourist-sportsman in his car will never know. Your feet may swell and blister, but many new wonderful sights come before the eyes when you are walking silently through the bush; and the mere absence of the usual trappings of a motorized safari, the tents, the tables and chairs, the convenient radio, creates a sense of freedom. From day to day you advance from one river or waterhole to the next, and at night, after they have eaten, the porters sit beside their fires and sing.

In the present case, of course, these idyllic scenes had been abruptly upset by the wounding of the elephant. Provided he is not hurt too badly, an elephant will travel thirty miles in a night, and now for five days the Commissioner had been chasing his quarry over very rough country indeed. There had been little time for eating or sleeping and matters were made a good deal worse by the hardness of the ground in this dry season, and the sparseness of the trees; the wounded beast was leaving few tracks in his wake. He might be glimpsed for a moment, but then he would vanish silently into the rocks on his great sponge feet. He had left the herd and was travelling alone, fast and erratically, so erratically indeed that many conflicting reports had come in from the tribesmen, and the Commissioner had been off on one wild goose chase after another. Now he was baffled. After a short rest at the camp he set off on his search again.

Blower, Longhurst, my wife, and myself meanwhile drove by truck down a rough track to the Kidepo River, which runs westward across the border into the Sudan and eventually reaches the swamps of the Upper Nile. This is a marvellous place to see wild game, and for some reason, perhaps because it is so seldom visited, the animals appeared to me to be exceptionally tame. The kongoni, in the usual way, had their sentinels mounted on the ant-heaps, to keep watch while the other antelopes in the herd were grazing, but they let us get very close indeed – sometimes within fifty yards – before they raised the alarm. Then in the general scatter one saw many pretty scenes; the ostriches stepping off, their scrawny heads turned backwards towards us as they ran, the undulating giraffes in clusters of a dozen or more, the wistful mooning buffaloes, the zebra, a special breed in these regions which, in the male, appears to have no name; and best of all perhaps, the oribi. The oribi is a sprightly little antelope of a *café-au-lait* colour and about the size of a greyhound. He proceeds, when in haste, like a hurdler with his feet tucked up beneath him each time he launches himself into a spring. When Longhurst shot one for our dinner it subsided with hardly a sigh. Only the little black-faced vervet monkeys seemed really afraid, and even they squeaked and chattered at us with annoyance once they regained the safety of the trees.

But it is the Kidepo River itself which is the really enchanting sight in this forgotten corner. At this time of the year (February) it is almost dry, and its banks are lined with colonnades of borassus palms which grow to a height of some thirty feet above the ground. The trunks of these palms are as clear-cut and symmetrical as polished marble, and at first sight they resemble nothing so much as the columns of a Doric temple; but then, coming closer, you see the dazzling white sand of the dry river-bed beyond and the arching fronds above, and the effect is not so much one of Greece as of Egypt, Luxor perhaps, and the colours are the colours of the Nile. Great orange-tinted fibrous fruit, the size and shape of a bowl in a bowling alley, hang in clusters, and occasionally one, over-ripe, comes crashing to the ground. The elephants love the huge berries, and Juma spoke highly of their flavour, but I found them gritty and dull.

A muddy greenish liquid which looks and feels and probably tastes like warm soup fills the depressions in the river-bed, and these are the natural meeting places of every living thing that flies, walks, hops, or crawls along the arid valley. The crocodile slithers into the ooze as you come down the bank, but the birds have stronger nerves, especially the marabous, which appear at all times to wear an aggrieved and petulant air. They stand morosely round the edges of the pools with their grey wings gathered round them as though they feel cold and are sheltering from the rain in the midst of this enervating heat. As you approach they walk away slowly and resentfully, and their take-off, which they delay until you are within a few yards, is an awkward effort, a lumbering run of a foot or two and an unsteady lurch into the air. They make a noise like an awning flapping in the wind. Then in a moment all the heaviness is gone. The bird flies with the fingered tips of its wings curved delicately upwards, and an effortless glide takes it over the tops of the palms. Compared to this performance even the flight of the heron or the ibis can be a laboured thing.

We found no signs of fire rings, and in fact we hardly expected to, for Blower had had his askaris patrolling the border regularly for the past twelve months. But this did not mean that the poachers had given up entirely. Instead they were reverting to the use of one of the oldest and cruellest snares in Africa, the wheel-trap. This consists of an ordinary wire noose which lies concealed on the ground and is attached to a heavy log. Beneath the noose, buried lightly under leaves and sticks, is a round wooden hoop about the size of a large dinner plate with spokes reaching inward. The whole contraption looks a little like the wheel of a child's bicycle, except that the sharp points of the spokes are not joined together in the centre. The idea is that an animal, preferably an elephant, should put one of its feet first through the noose and then through the wooden wheel. It sounds an improbable device, but in practice it works very well; the spokes of the wheel dig in around the flesh of the animal's leg and hold the noose in place above. An elephant dragging a heavy log cannot go very far, and if he is lucky he is soon followed and speared to death. One says lucky because if he is not found he drags the log around for many days or even weeks while the snare and the wire noose cut into his flesh and he dies slowly in great pain.

Blower explained to me that he hoped to stop a good deal of this cruel trapping by permitting tribal hunts to take place when the game was plentiful. Something had to be done to appease the Africans' desperate hunger for meat, and these hunts were the best method, provided they were properly controlled. He had organized one such hunt only a few days before, he said, and it had been a great success. When the tribesmen were assembled with their spears it was explained that certain rare animals were not to be molested, and that there was to be a limit to the numbers killed. Then the warriors spread themselves around a promising-looking area of bush and began beating it systematically in towards the centre. Apparently it had been an exciting day. A Karamojong can run as fast as an antelope, and whenever an oribi or a kongoni got up the young men dashed at it, hurling their spears as they went along, missing for the most part, but bringing the animal down in the end. Some scores of beasts had been killed, and Blower thought that would be enough to keep the tribesmen happy for a long time to come. The meat is seldom eaten raw but instead is dried in strips and when it is salted keeps indefinitely.

There was news of the wounded elephant when we got back to camp. Some villagers had come in from the neighbouring hills saying that it had been browsing around their village all day. No one knew where the District Commissioner had gone, and so Blower's askari sergeant, now fit as a lion, was sent off with a rifle through the midday heat to finish off the beast. Presently one of the askaris came in and said that he had heard a shot, and it was soon after this that the Commissioner himself returned. He was understandably dismayed. The ivory would be his, even though he had not killed the elephant, but that was not the point. He had a passion for elephants. He had hunted them for years, and it was a matter of pride as well as humanity that he himself should follow up and kill any beast he had wounded. And now, after six days' fruitless slogging over the mountains, to find that the quarry had been loitering hardly a mile or two away, and had fallen to another rifle while he himself was wandering off in the wrong direction – this was a little bitter.

However, there was now a great stir in the camp, for a dead elephant meant meat unlimited. Mysteriously, out of the bush, all kinds of Africans appeared, men, women, and children, all carrying tins, bowls, gourds, anything that would serve to bring the meat away. They fell into line in Indian file and with the whole cavalcade at his back the Commissioner set off in the tracks of the sergeant. The sun was still high enough to penetrate the bush with a close stifling heat, and there was no sound except for the breaking of twigs and branches and the expectant murmuring of the Karamojong following on behind. After half an hour the procession stopped to listen. There was still no sound. The sergeant's tracks were there, but he seemed to have vanished as effectively as the elephant itself. One of the tribesmen lifted a horn to his mouth and blew a high long note; but there was still no reply and the commissioner pushed on again. At the end of an hour even the best of Blower's trackers had to admit that they were lost. Then finally, in the casual and haphazard way things happen in Africa, word spread along the column that there was no one there who had actually seen the elephant in the morning, and that quite possibly the whole story was a rumour. As for the sound of the shot being heard no one could be quite sure of it any longer. Once again the horn was sounded, and when it brought no response there seemed to be nothing more to be done; the procession turned round and trooped back to camp.

I myself missed this excursion, for Dr Longhurst had kindly invited me to make a flight with him to watch the wild game from the air and at that moment we were cruising over the Kidepo Valley. Perhaps cruising is not quite the right word. Dr Longhurst was a fighter-pilot in the war, and now in the miniscule two-seater, tossed by a bumpy wind, we dived, turned, and zoomed back into the sky again, and Dr Longhurst was happy. He banked sharply, came down to 200 feet, reduced speed to just over stalling point (which was 45 m.p.h.), gripped the joystick with his knees, opened the window, tested the light with a meter, took out a camera with a telescopic lens, and began taking pictures of giraffe. It was not reckless – he was a wonderful pilot – it was just intensely surprising. The view, I must admit, was extraordinary. There were far more animals about than I had realized when on the ground, and the valleys were criss-crossed with hundreds of game trails. Not only the giraffe were running beneath us but mobs of zebra, topi, kongoni, Grant's gazelle, oribi, buffalo, and ostriches as well, all of them catching the sunlight in a different way, raising different trails of dust, weaving in and out of each other, and making changing patterns on the sand. It was very beautiful, and at the same time very unnatural. The animals were not running as they normally do; none could precisely locate the centre of the hellish noise above, and so they charged blindly in every direction, heading mostly for the open.

In many parts of Africa now wild animals have grown so used to aircraft that they hardly bother to look up any more. But here the noise was a bewildering thing. I spotted one big rhinoceros out in the open and he stood like a bulldog. He was ready for fight but he could not make out where the danger was threatening. He charged first one way, then another, and then wheeled round suddenly as though he was being attacked in the rear. It was not fair to agitate him so much and we flew away.

Longhurst was doing a year's tour in Africa on a Fullbright scholarship, and his special studies were the hippopotamus and the buffalo. He had been having some awkward experiences in the Queen Elizabeth Park, at the other end of Uganda, where he was dissecting hippopotami in an attempt to learn something of their life cycle and their habits. Cutting up a hippopotamus is an extensive operation even in the best of circumstances, but it was made much more difficult, he said, by the frenzy of the Africans to get at the meat. Directly he shot a specimen and towed it to the bank a huge crowd was sure to gather. He had tried keeping them back with ropes and the local police, and once he had fired a shot over their heads. But it made little difference, the sight of the heavy spongy flesh had been too much; the meat was snatched off the scales as he was weighing it and surgery had to be carried out through a barrage of clutching hands.

Hippopotami multiply like rabbits where they are protected, and they lay the land waste when they come ashore to browse at night and wallow in the mud-holes. It is Longhurst's contention – and he holds to it strongly – that you cannot allow wild animals to proliferate like this to the detriment not only of human beings but of other animals and perhaps themselves as well; consequently, he wants to kill off a reasonable number of game every year and to control the remainder – in short, to farm wild animals precisely as domestic animals are farmed. This he thinks is their only hope of survival: to turn them into a commercial enterprise. In the Queen Elizabeth Park, where the hippopotamus population has now risen to something like 14,000 (a census is difficult), he would kill off thirty per cent, establish a slaughterhouse, and sell the meat to the Africans at the current market price of about two shillings a pound. Some of the profits would go to the local African communities and some to the parks and game reserves, the main idea behind all this being to interest the Africans (who presumably will take over the government one day) in the commercial value of wild life, not only as a means of attracting tourists, but, quite simply, as butcher's meat. In Longhurst's view, there simply isn't enough room even in Africa for wild animals to roam wild any more. The land is needed for agriculture.

It is a theory which is much discussed among ecologists now, and it has its opponents, principally among the people who do not agree that human interests should always triumph over every other living thing on earth. They point out that most of the wild animals in Africa (and everywhere else for that matter) have already been wantonly destroyed, and that the remainder are still fighting a losing battle for survival. Moreover, they like wild animals the way they are – wild. They don't want them to be tame like cattle, and they believe that there is still plenty of land in Africa which can be reserved for them. The whole point of the parks and game reserves, they argue, is to preserve the land and the animals in their natural state. The hunting lion, the herds of elephants, the migrations of antelopes – these are some of the last great natural spectacles left in the world, and they have a fascination which is beyond the value of profits from butcher's meat. As for the danger of a species getting out of hand and becoming too numerous, nature herself always has a way of correcting these things, through famine and by other means. It is dangerous to disturb this process; you might kill off ten thousand hippopotami only to discover that disease demolishes the rest.

And so the argument revolves; on the one side those who are rudely known as 'the butchers' and on the other the 'sentimentalists'. And wandering somewhere in and out of both these camps is the hunter, the serious hunter like our District Commissioner, who wants to preserve the game for sport, and who in an odd way treasures the creatures he destroys.

When we got back to camp from our flight there was more news of the elephant. He had been seen heading for the Sudan border where he could not be followed without a special permit from the Sudanese, and the Commissioner was hastily preparing to set out again. Longhurst planned to make another flight in the morning, and he promised to send a message if he spotted the animal. The Commissioner was to reveal his position on the ground by firing a purple verey light into the sky, and then a message giving the elephant's whereabouts was to be parachuted down to him from the plane.

All this seemed to be of the greatest importance to us at the time, and I remember how we sat up at night debating the chances of the next day's hunt, and how we talked of the poaching and the fire rings and the tribal fights. But there never seems to be a clear-cut end to anything in Africa. When my wife and I left Opotipot the plane was still flying about, the Commissioner was still searching through the scrub, and the elephant was still wandering about somewhere in the hills waiting to keep his inevitable appointment with death.

CHAPTER EIGHT

SINCE MAYERLING

NOTHING now will persuade the people of Kenya that the hydrogen bomb, the sputniks, or some other artificial agency has not upset the climate of Africa. Year after year they used to have their two dry seasons and their two wet ones, and you could name the start and the end of these seasons almost to a day. This was of some importance, since in many parts of Kenya you cannot move far off the beaten track, or sometimes even on the track itself, once rain begins to fall. But in the past three years storms have burst out of the clear sky in even the driest months. It was a dismal sight in February seeing the big-game hunters sitting in the Nairobi hotels. Most of them had flown in from the other side of the world and had planned their trips for many months in advance knowing that in East Africa it never rains in February. And now the rain poured down, and rain can be really depressing when you are paying safari fees of something like £35 a day waiting for it to stop. Others who had succeeded in getting out of town were, if anything, rather worse off, they simply sat in their tents in the mud and not all the money in the world could get them out.

I myself had my own reasons for being dismayed by the weather, for I was also waiting to set out on my safari to Lake Rudolf. My wife and I had planned with a friend, a white hunter named Sidney Downey, to make this trip, not in order to shoot or to photograph, but simply because we were beguiled by the idea of the place. For Downey it was to be a busman's holiday, as he wanted to investigate the condition of the wild life in the area; for us it was exploration pure and simple.

Lake Rudolf lies in wild and desolate country in the north-western corner of Kenya on the Abyssinian border, and parts of the eastern shore are absolute desert. Although it covers an area of 3,500 square miles (which makes it the twenty-third largest lake in the world), and is some 180 miles long by 20 to 40 miles wide, no ship ever sails there and hardly a village of any size exists along the shore. Few people ever go to Lake Rudolf, and the whole region has become doubly isolated in recent years because there has been a certain amount of tribal fighting at the Abyssinian end of the lake, and the British authorities in Kenya have declared it a restricted area – a place where no visitors are allowed except by special permit.

Everything we heard about the place seemed interesting. It was said to be a great bird sanctuary, and the fishing was declared to be stupendous. Yet the lake was drying up. A considerable river, the Omo, flowed in from the Abyssinian mountains, and there were other seasonal streams as well, but none of this intake was able to keep pace with the excessive evaporation. The level of the water had gone down thirty feet since 1914, and the Sudanese who had once owned a strip of the shore in the extreme north were now left high and dry in the sand. One of the effects of this evaporation had been to create a strong deposit of natron salt in the water, and while this was apparently excellent for hippopotami and crocodiles human beings found it a gloomy and depressing drink.

Then there were the inhabitants. These were the Turkana, a warrior-pastoralist tribe who were still living in a state of nature and were practically untouched by the outside world. This last was the thing that seemed to have most impressed other visitors to the lake; its isolation, its extreme sense of detachment and loneliness. It was as if the Dead Sea had been transported, enormously enlarged, into the midst of equatorial Africa and then abandoned and forgotten.

Hearing these things we were naturally impatient to get on the road. But February turned into March and still intermittent showers fell. We were staying with friends outside Nairobi, and each evening I used to watch the rain clouds banking up over the Ngong hills to the east. There was another ominous sign that there was more bad weather ahead; the African villagers who are supposed to have a sixth sense about the elements were starting to burn off their grazing lands so that the new grass would sprout up more rapidly in the wet. Every morning there was a fresh damp smell of burning in the air.

But then abruptly, in the middle of March, when normally heavy rain was due to start at any moment, the weather improved. We decided to wait no longer; early one morning we packed up two trucks with camping gear and set out. We had planned to make for a place called Ferguson's Gulf on the western shore of the lake (thus avoiding the deserts to the south and east), and this meant a two to four days' journey from Nairobi depending on how many of the river crossings had been washed out. For the first day our route lay north-westwards as far as the Uganda border, a spectacular drive, since you cross the Great Rift Valley and then on the Equator mount up to nine thousand feet. At Kitale, which lies under Mount Elgon, you run through some of the loveliest country in all Africa, dairy farms and crops that are as green as anything in England. Thence the track takes you directly to the north, and almost at once plunges down two steep escarpments which are as hot and dry as Arizona. At three thousand feet above sea level we started peeling off our sweaters, and at two thousand we were in a semi-desert with red dust and sand flying up in clouds behind us. It was the sort of contrast which normally you only experience when you make a rapid air journey to another country. In place of the great groves of eucalyptus and the lush fields which we had left only a few miles behind we were now bumping over dried-up river-beds lined with Dom palms, and enormous rose-coloured anthills sprouted up on every side. This is the country where the oryx runs, an antelope whose long straight corrugated horns stick up like spears. But we saw none. The animals we did see had a kind of desert-domesticity about them; small grey shaggy camels, donkeys with a black stripe like a collar round their necks, numberless goats. Mongooses scampered like cats across the track, and even the ostriches were small and had a tame and wearied air. The prevailing colour of the flat landscape was dusty olive-grey, but the bright things that caught our eyes were inexpressibly bright : scarlet beetles and lizards with vermilion eyes, tropical butterflies and sunbirds with iridescent wings darting among the dry twigs.

We made good time, and already on the second night reached a British outpost called Lodwar, only forty miles from the lake. Twenty years ago places like Lodwar were two a penny on the map, and if one did not know them from personal experience they were made familiar enough by such movies as *Beau Geste* and the *King of the Khyber Rifles*. The fort stands on rising ground with the Union Jack (or possibly the French tricolour) flying above in a pale blue sky. An appalling waste of sand and stark rocks lies round about, and camels are squatting under the palms by a water-hole. In the compound of the fort itself a squad of soldiers is drilling; others stand sentry in the watchtowers looking out over the desert, and in the early morning a bugle sounds.

At Lodwar these scenes are preserved with an almost painful thoroughness, and with a sudden shock one realizes there that they have become as out of date as the illustrations in old Victorian adventure books. It seems incredible that the camel-driver and the native soldier in his képi (with a flap at the back to keep the sun off) should have become anachronisms so completely and so quickly. One feels one knows these people and this fort just as well as one once knew some household, some garden, where one played as a child, as well as one knew the cupboard where the toy soldiers and the hockey sticks were kept. One knows all the manners and the customs of the place; the salutes, the flag being lowered at sunset, and the bugler who sounds the recall with that same authority with which once the gong was rung to call us in for dinner. It is very queer and a little disturbing.

I found myself recalling every detail with an almost Proustian clarity, and, I remembered, with a curious sense of embarrassment, how important all these things once were to me, how I gobbled them up in the movies and the adventure books. And now that I had arrived at the reality of them at Lodwar, it was the reality, and not the fiction, that was unreal.

Lodwar, however, provided a fine outpostish sort of atmosphere from which to launch ourselves, like explorers, on the final stage of our trip. We had a comfortable night in the District Commissioner's house, and, rising with the bugle, we set off again.

Although only forty miles divided us from Ferguson's Gulf on the lake it seemed to me to be an interminable journey, much longer than anything that had gone before. There were moments when our trucks bowled along at thirty miles an hour over gravelled salt pans as smooth as the tarmac on an airfield; but then the landscape degenerated into plains of hot broken basalt and heavy sand. Nothing but withered thorn scrub seemed able to grow (although Downey, who had been a soldier in these parts during the war, assured me that with the first touch of rain even the deadest-looking log on the ground would burst into green leaf). Occasionally some antelope like the Grant's gazelle, which seldom drinks (it manages to absorb moisture from the plants it eats), would poise for an instant on the track and then bound off into the mirage on the skyline like a dolphin leaping in the sea. Presently the temperature rose to 99 degrees, and of the lake itself there was no sign whatever. In this way two or three hours went by. Then in one instant there occurred a slight freshening of the atmosphere, the suggestion of a breeze. The temperature dropped to 94 degrees and we wound our way through the last sand dunes to the shore.

This sudden apparition of the lake has been best described by Count Samuel Teleki and Lieutenant Ludwig von Höhnel, the first two white men ever to set eyes on it. They began their expedition into the interior from Mombasa just seventy years ago, and they had a frightful time. It was one of those horrendous African journeys which once seemed just as strange and fateful as the present attempts to reach outer space. For a year they wandered about with a retinue of two hundred porters, and they were half-starved and often half-dead with sickness and thirst. Just why two prosperous Hungarian gentlemen should have chosen to do this remains something a mystery. The story runs that Count Teleki came to Africa because he was mixed up in some scandal at the court of the Emperor Franz Josef in Vienna, but a much more probable explanation seems to be that, like most African explorers from Livingstone onwards, he and his companion were seized with a vision of distant unknown eldorados – this, and the simple satisfaction of walking through country no civilized man had ever seen before. The local tribes spoke of a great lake to the north, the Basso Narok or Black Lake, and that was enough to lead them on. At all events, on 5 March 1888, they sighted their goal at last.

'For a long time,' Ludwig von Höhnel wrote afterwards, 'we gazed with speechless delight, spellbound by the beauty of the scene before us, while our men, equally silent, stared into the distance for a few minutes, to break presently into shouts of astonishment at the sight of the glittering expanse of the great lake which melted on the horizon into the blue of the sky. At that moment all our dangers, all our fatigue were forgotten in the joy of finding our exploring expedition crowned with success at last. Full of enthusiasm and gratefully remembering the gracious interest taken in our plans from the first by his Royal Highness, Prince Rudolf of Austria, Count Teleki named the sheet of water, set like a pearl of great price in the wonderful landscape before us, Lake Rudolf.'

As with all else on this desperate journey there was, of course, an anti-climax: 'The men rushed down shouting, to plunge into the lake, but soon returned in bitter disappointment; the water was brackish!'

They were obliged to drink it, however, and then Teleki and his companion turned north and discovered another smaller lake, the Basso-Na-Ebor, or White Lake, which they named Stephanie after Rudolf's wife, the daughter of the King of the Belgians.

If Rudolf himself was ever aware of the honours he had little time to enjoy them. Hardly a year had elapsed when on 30 January 1889, he and his mistress, Baroness Marie Vetsera, were found dead together in a hunting lodge at Mayerling in the woods outside Vienna. Fate has been unkind to the last to his unfortunate wife Stephanie; her lake has now dried up and hardly a swamp remains.

Lake Rudolf, being much larger and deeper, cannot have changed very much since the days of Mayerling, so far as one can make out from von Höhnel's admirable description of his journey (published in English in two massive volumes in 1894). The things he saw seventy years ago we now saw again. A strong breeze was stirring up the water into white-crested waves, and all the shore was fringed with wading and swimming birds. Overhead a great cloud of flamingoes, disturbed by our arrival, kept dissolving and reforming in shades of pinkish black and white. As Downey got out his gun to shoot a duck or two a group of naked Turkana boys came running towards us, and they followed him like dogs into the reeds. His first shot seemed to set the whole sky into a commotion; all at once the air was filled with many different kinds of duck, with white egrets and black darters, with pelicans, Egyptian geese, herons, storks, and cormorants. They soon settled, however, since hardly anyone now shoots along the lake, and as Downey aimed again the Turkana boys kept frisking through the water to bring the dead ducks to the shore. These boys were astonishing swimmers. They grinned and shouted as they swam, and when they leapt out on to the bank with the water streaming from their bodies they looked as though they had been painted with shining black enamel.

We had stopped the truck close to a small village of grass huts, and now there gathered round us a crowd of immensely lithe slim men wearing close-fitting caps made of upswept feathers from the breasts of pelicans – just these and a few beads and nothing else. The women, standing a little to one side but gradually edging their way forward, were precisely as von Höhnel described them; some wearing vee-shaped aprons sewn with broken pieces of ostrich egg-shells, others with the skins of animals round their waists and coils of wire around their necks and arms, others again smeared with grease and white ashes; and all of them were heavily marked with self-inflicted scars about their shoulders. I thought them much better-looking than their sisters of the Karamojong tribe who live just across the Uganda border to the west. The babies too looked healthier, and there were none so small that did not sport at least one string of beads around the neck. These beads, incidentally, run in fashions; those we saw were mainly red and gold, but in the previous year, we were told, everyone preferred gold and white.

These lakeside Turkana are the real primitives of Africa – not primitive in the sense of being crude or brutish, they were very far from that – but in their loyalty to their ancient tribal customs. They do not drift from their villages; their entire world is bounded by what we could see here on the lake, and there was nothing here that belonged to the twentieth century or indeed any other country in recorded history. The tribe was in the permanent state of its nativity.

Some of the Turkana's practices might be brutal by civilized standards – they leave the sick and the very old outside the villages to die – but in the main they are gentle sensible people, and it would be quite unfair to blame them for their backwardness. They have no boats but that is because there is no timber here with which to build them. Instead they make rafts of the Kon-Tiki kind by lashing the trunks of the Dom palms together. These vessels become waterlogged and sink after a time but they serve the fishermen very well. They have no iron for hooks, but their own methods of catching fish are quite effective. They weave a semi-circular basket of wood and fibre, about five foot in circumference, open at the bottom, and with this they wade into the shallow water. The basket is plunged downward at random on to the mud at the bottom, and if a fish has been caught it can be felt lunging about inside the wickerwork; it can easily be dragged out. The fish are then cleaned and slit open and either dried in the sun or smoked beside a fire. When a sufficient quantity has been prepared the catch is bundled up like so many pieces of buckled cardboard and carried away on the heads of the women; and although they smell to high heaven (the women, alas, as well as the fish), they provide the Turkana with enough proteins to enable them to survive in a hard environment where there is nothing much for their cattle to feed on except the weeds along the lake. A warrior will eat ten pounds of fish in a day if he can get it. Sometimes his hunger will drive him out on moonless nights. Then he takes a flaming torch made of palm leaves bound tightly together, and with spear and basket waits for the fish to come swimming towards him in the shallows.

All these people were delighted to see us. This is one of the pleasantest things about travelling in out-of-the-way places in Africa now. In the more settled areas the clothed and partly-educated African has, as a rule, a subdued appearance, but a certain hostility is nearly always there, hidden but pervasive. Here in the wilds it is the other way about. The tribesmen look fierce at first, but you soon discover that they accept the whites with naïve and implicit trust. Often on this journey we would come suddenly upon a group of them walking in single file through the scrub, each man with a spear or two in his hand, and they had the aspect of complete savagery. But then invariably they smiled, and lifting their hands in a casual salute called out to us the word *Jambo*, which is something more than 'Hullo', for it is a warm and genuine greeting.

So now the Turkana came pressing forward to unload the trucks, and although our boat was a cockleshell affair that lurched frantically in the waves they soon had it packed expertly with our baggage. Then they rowed and shoved and dragged us to a spit of land on the other side of the bay where a camp of grass huts had been built among the palms. As we touched dry land on the other side the crocodiles slithered away off the bank into the warm brown water.

There was something of the atmosphere of the South Pacific islands about this camp, and we felt it very strongly when we got ashore. It was enchanting and at the same time very queer, rather as though one had set out for the Canadian lakes and had arrived at Hawaii by mistake. Yet here it all was: the heavy soporific air, the palm-leaf huts, the teeming birds and the fish, the sound of the waves on the beach and the yellow sand under one's bare toes. We had crocodiles instead of sharks, and the mooning hippopotamus in place of the sea-cow or the dugong, but all the other effects were of coral reefs and the tropical sea. The moon here, near the Equator, is very close and very bright. In the early mornings we used to walk down to the edge of the water and see where, during the night, the crocodiles had dug their claws into the wet sand as they came ashore; and always there was an intricate network of footprints made by many different birds. These, with the droppings and the fallen feathers and the bones of fish, made a series of abstract patterns on the beach, and they were not unlike paintings in prehistoric caves.

The crocodile grows on one. In all Africa no living thing, except possibly the hyena, is so much loathed, and yet the more you know this monster the more interesting he becomes. Herodotus appears to have been the first traveller in Africa to have observed the crocodile really well, and he speaks of it without any rancour whatever. 'Of all known animals,' he says in his famous passage on the subject, 'this is the one which from the smallest size grows to be the greatest; for the egg of the crocodile is but little bigger than a goose's egg; yet when it is full grown the animal measures frequently seventeen cubits and even more.' A cubit being the distance from a man's elbow to the tip of his middle finger, a distance say of about 20 inches, this makes the full-grown crocodile about 28 feet long, which is big but not impossible. Like so many other reptiles, the crocodile may well have grown smaller since Herodotus first observed it, or at any rate heard about it, on the lower Nile some 2,400 years ago. He goes on to note that, unlike other animals, the crocodile has no tongue, and that it can move only one of its jaws. And he adds :

'As it lives chiefly in the river, it has the inside of its mouth constantly covered with leeches; hence it happens that, while all the other birds and beasts avoid it, with the trochilus (or tick-bird) it lives at peace since it owes much to that bird : for the crocodile, when he leaves the water and comes out upon the land, is in the habit of lying with his mouth wide open, facing the western breeze; at such times the trochilus goes into his mouth and devours the leeches. This benefits the crocodile, who is pleased, and takes care not to hurt the trochilus.'

One cannot, of course, be absolutely certain whether or not a crocodile is pleased, and I have seen them many times facing other directions than the west; but the rest of the description is an accurate account of what one sees along the more remote African lakes and rivers today. Crocodiles are diminishing fairly rapidly, since hardly any-where in Africa are there any game laws to protect them, and all human beings approach them in much the same way as they approach snakes; with an instinctive desire to kill. They are described as vermin, and most sportsmen almost automatically will take a pot shot whenever they catch a crocodile unawares on a sandbank, or even when they see only the two glaring eyes and the snout projecting above the surface of the water. They do this not because they want the meat (crocodile flesh is foul), or the skin, which is most difficult to remove, but with a gratifying sense of duty; no less than St George himself they are removing an evil dragon from the earth.

Sir Winston Churchill put the matter very well in an account of a journey he made down the Nile fifty years ago; 'As we were thus scrambling along the brink of the river a crocodile was discovered basking in the sunshine on a large rock in midstream, about a hundred and fifty yards from the shore. I avow, with what regrets may be necessary, an active hatred of these brutes and a desire to kill them. It was a tempting shot, for the ruffian lay sleeping in the sun-blaze, his mouth wide open and his fat and scaly flanks exposed. Two or three attendant white birds hopped about him ... I fired. What the result of the shot may have been I do not know, for the crocodile gave one leap of mortal agony or surprise and disappeared in the water.'

Then there is the commercial motive. Crocodile fishing organizations have sprung up in many parts of East Africa, and their methods very much resemble those described by Herodotus : 'They bait a hook with a chine of pork and let the meat be carried out into the middle of the stream, while the hunter on the bank holds a living pig, which he belabours. The crocodile hears its cries, and, making for the sound, encounters the pork, which he instantly swallows down. The men on the shore haul, and when they have got him to land, the first thing the hunter does is to plaster his eyes with mud. This once accomplished, the animal is dispatched with ease, otherwise he gives great trouble.'

I have never seen a modern crocodile fisherman belabouring a pig or plastering a crocodile's eyes with mud, but hook and bait remain much the same as they were in Herodotus's time. On the upper Nile they have simpler methods. The hunters go out at night carrying a bright light in their boats, and the crocodiles, either mesmerized by the glare or simply curious, swim towards them. They are easily seen, for their eyes shine red at night. When they come near enough the hunters bash their heads in with an axe. Most of the hides go to France to be made into women's handbags.

The consequence of all this is that crocodiles are no more seen for a thousand miles or more on the lower Nile, and even on the great central lakes they are becoming rare. But not on Lake Rudolf, where they are seldom hunted. Often I counted half a dozen or more cruising around us when we went out in the boat. Normally one associates crocodiles with swamps and quiet lagoons, and it was strange to see them here in rough water during a storm. They look like logs or even derelict fishing boats as the waves break over their backs, and when they lie on the beach the surf comes streaming off their scaly hides like a waterfall pouring over a ledge of rock.

We were astonished at the way the Turkana boys jumped into these dangerous waters, but we were assured that the lake is so full of fish that the crocodiles are replete and have no wish to attack. Naturally at first one accepts this with a certain reserve. Yet in the end we found ourselves bathing – at all events in the shallow water a yard or two from the shore – several times a day, and in the hot night, when the heavy woolly heat pressed on one like a warm coat worn in summer, we dragged our camp-beds down to the beach and slept there without disturbance.

We were told a story about the myriad birds on the lake that interested me. Once, apparently, they had been fewer in numbers. This was because a celebrated sportsman had arrived one day, a prince from Central Europe. In the course of a single morning this man brought down some 600 sand-grouse in the plains beyond the lake, and then he came down to the lake itself to shoot the ducks along the shore. The Turkana still spoke of the occasion with awe. It is not often in Africa that the tribesmen kill wild game for the sake of killing unless there is some mortal danger, some superstition or some tribal rite involved. When they have got enough to eat they stop; and that also is the law of the jungle among the predatory animals themselves. So now, when this Bwana went on and on killing ducks by the hundred – more than enough for everyone to eat – the tribesmen could only suppose that he was trying to placate some strange tormented white man's demon of his own. They were by no means critical of this, they respected it, even though for a time afterwards the ducks disappeared from this corner of the lake. The game laws of Kenya were altered after this little jaunt so as to limit a sportsman's daily bag, and the Prince, it was said, went on to the Congo, where he continued to shoot 'not for the pot but for the bag'.

My wife and I had already heard about the Prince on

our way from Nairobi. He was described as a delightful man, with charming and considerate manners. He had the reputation of being an enthusiastic naturalist.

The moral in all this seems to be that you can make no rules about killing even though it is a theme that never deserts you for long in Africa. In Lodwar we had seen a prison filled with Mau Mau terrorists who had been sent there to serve their sentences well away from the more settled parts of Kenya. These men had taken an oath to kill and by the most brutal means imaginable. Yet they looked mild enough to me as they sat there squatting in the sunshine behind the barbed wire, as mild as the Turkana who killed, not for hate, but for food, as mild as the Prince who shot 'for the bag', as mild even as my friend Sidney Downey, who, like so many others in Kenya, has spent a lifetime hunting, but who shoots now only occasionally, and not for the kill but for the pleasure of the stalking.

The mornings were magical. Long before the sun appeared a green light slanted across the lake from the east, and through this the pelicans came flying. They flew in batches of anything from five to fifty birds, and either in a vee formation or in line, but always with one bird leading. They gave one the impression that they were ascending and descending a series of invisible hills in the sky. When they flapped their wings, a lazy casual motion, they rose together in a line; then together they went into a long glide which almost took them to the surface of the lake. Then again in unison they flapped and rose like galleons from the waves. Often one would see as many as a thousand birds flapping and gliding in this way, and their wings made a pleasant sighing in the air. They landed a little awkwardly, like elderly gentlemen stepping off a moving bus.

By day they fished. They came cruising out from the shore with the appearance of a miniature fleet of sailing boats. Sometimes, apparently at the direction of some old male, they formed a circle, and with a queer hissing noise, a sound like *whiss whiss whiss*, sought to drive the shoals of fish into the centre. But more often they moved in small squadrons, sailing in line astern. Every few moments one would see a bird suddenly bring his long beak backward and downward until it lay horizontal with the surface of the water and just an inch or two above it. Then, like an arrow from a bow, like a harpoon leaving a fisherman's gun, the beak shot forward in a smooth, very swift lunge. One expected to see a fish impaled, but instead there was a long pause while the bird, his bill now pointing downward vertically into the water, appeared to be quietly meditating. Then at last, with a quick upward flick of the head the bill was raised into the air and as the bird gobbled once or twice one could see the shape of the fish slipping down his throat into his stomach.

Only darkness put an end to these labours. Then once again one saw the great dark frieze of birds in the sky as they made off to a sandy promontary just beyond our camp, and there, murmuring, clucking, and complaining, they settled for the night. Each different species of bird appeared to have its own chosen roosting place – the ducks in the reeds, the herons in the palms, the fish eagles on the bushes, the flamingoes on the shore – and if there were predators among them, birds that preyed on other birds, I never saw them. The one consuming interest of every bird along the lake, indeed of almost every living thing, was fish.

The sheer mass of fish was fabulous. They boiled up around us in huge shoals wherever we moved in the boat, often barely a dozen yards from the shore. We caught fish, ate fish, smelt fish, and saw fish jumping from the early morning until the moon rose at night; and there were times when one began to feel like a fish oneself, caught in a vast aquarium filled with wet silver fins and goggling eyes. There were three main varieties: the tiger fish, a tremendous fighter, looked like a young shark about eighteen inches long. It had cruel backward-slanting teeth and was not much good to eat. Then there were the *Tilapia nilotica* and the *Tilapia galilaea*, that same fish which was caught by Christ and the disciples in the Sea of Galilee. It runs for the most part to about five or six pounds in weight, and is the staple diet of the lakeside Turkana. Finally there was the Nile perch. This really is a phenomenal monster. One hears so many tales about it that the truth becomes a little elusive. It is certain, however, that it is one of the largest freshwater fishes in existence, and that a 160-lb. specimen that was landed in the Nile recently is not a record; even the earliest explorers speak of much better catches than this.* Not a great deal is known yet about the Nile perch. It seems to breed in Lake Albert in Uganda, and then makes its way down the Nile as far as Khartoum, several thousand miles away. Anglers at Rhino Camp, just below Lake Albert, have noticed that the fish appear to move in age-groups; thus one day you strike a shoal of twenty-pounders and on the next they run to forty pounds or more. But the fish does not breed only in the Nile; it can be found in abundance here on Lake Rudolf and at many other places. In the Sudan the tribesmen sit on the rocks above the cataracts and shoot the bigger specimens with bows and arrows as they leap into the air on their return journey upstream.

The more usual method of catching them, however, is the one we employed here : trolling from a boat. You let out about thirty yards of a strong line with a metal spinner on the end. When the strike comes it is not particularly spectacular; as a rule, the fish does not jump into the air but sounds at once. Usually it can be turned after forty or fifty yards of line have run out, and there then begins a series of slow rushes and retreats which may go on for anything up to half an hour or more before the fish is brought in. This at any rate was my own experience when I pulled in a twenty-one-pounder one night. It came out of the water like an old boot, and although I could see that such a tiddler did not count for very much with the two Turkana fishermen who were with us, they were pleased

* Captain Pitman informs me that 'the largest Nile perch caught on rod and line in the Lake Albert region weighed 226 lb. Monsters weighing 336 lb. and 360 lb. have also been netted there. All the huge fish are females, the males rarely exceeding 45 lb. in weight.'

because I was pleased, and we rowed home in a glow of mutual self-esteem. The singularity of the Nile perch, apart from its size and rapacity – apparently it will devour anything – is that a goliath the size of a man is just as good to eat as a ten-pounder.

So then, at Lake Rudolf an endless war is made against the fish. The crocodiles snap them up in the depths, the Turkana spear them and trap them in the shallows, the birds snatch them from the surface, and as though this were not enough the tiger fish eats the humble plankton-eating *Tilapia* and the Nile perch eats the tiger fish. Yet nothing seems to make any real inroad upon that spawning horde. It was marvellous to see what happened one evening when we paid out a net from the beach. At least a dozen Turkana tribesmen were required to drag it in, and they made a fine sight straining together on the lines, with the sunset light on their naked black bodies. Long before the net was gathered to the shore the fish began leaping frantically into the air and some escaped. But this did not matter in the least; some five hundred large *Tilapia* were presently spilled out on to the sand. The smaller fry, that is to say anything less than three- or four-pounders, were thrown back, along with the tiger fish and other strange denizens the names of which I will never know. The rest were threaded through the gills on a long fibre rope and towed off to a sort of fish-factory among the sand dunes, where they were cleaned, salted, and laid out for the sun to dry.

Otters, turtles, and even small crocodiles are sometimes brought in by the net and once a hippopotamus got entangled, creating havoc before he got away. But usually it is just more fish.

A retired British naval officer, Commander Dennis McKay, and his wife have made a home at Ferguson's Gulf, and they are the only white people who live on the lake. They were away when we first arrived, but they returned a day or two later and we went up to see them in the group of palm-leaf huts which they have built on a low sandy cliff above the lake. I was curious to meet them. It is a difficult thing for white people to live alone in Central Africa, especially in such an out-of-the-way backwater as this. The primitiveness of the country may be very stimulating to travellers, but it is quite another thing to live with it day after day. It presses on you and it can become quite over-powering at times, even to a transient.

The McKays made this matter very clear at once. Already for many years the Commander had served as the District Commissioner at Lodwar, so he knew the country, and both of them had the habit of isolation. When the problem of retirement came up, where were they to go? Back to England which had changed very much during the long period they had been abroad? Or here to the lake where the climate, hot though it was, suited them very well? It was very far from beach-combing. The Commander had set up a fishing business, and he had a governent contract to supply fish to the old men and women among the Turkana who otherwise would be left to starve and die. He and his wife had made themselves reasonably comfortable : they had a truck with which they fetched fresh drinking water from the plains beyond the lake, a fibre-glass motor-boat, a frigidaire that ran on kerosene, a staff of servants, canned food to supplement the fish, their books, and occasionally visitors.

Yet when all this was said it still seemed to me that there was something unexplained; some special qualification was needed to enable a man and a woman to live, if not cut off entirely from civilization, at least a good way removed from it. After a day or two with them I began to under-stand. They had achieved something which is very rare among white people in Central Africa : they accepted it. Without losing their own identity, they lived with the country on its own terms. They were absorbed in the minutiae of the extraordinary African life that was going on around them; they went with the weather and the wind. When a storm was about to blow up – and the lake storms can be cyclonic at times – the Commander knew the exact moment to make for the shore; he observed not the waves but the sandstorm blowing towards him along the coast. He knew his Turkana tribesmen with the sort of intimacy that can only come through a long series of shared experiences. He was living, in fact, as the head-man of his own village, and quite clearly he and his wife were very much liked. They themselves had trained many of the men since they were children, had taught them to handle the boats and the nets. They had bound up the leg of a boy who was so savagely bitten in the leg by a crocodile that he must have died had he been a white man, and had seen how, within three weeks, the patient was bounding about the village again. (This story made us move our beds a little higher up the beach that night.) They had sailed out to an uninhabited island in the lake, a thing practically no one has done because of the sudden storms; and had seen there the craters of extinct volcanoes and a few goats and a deserted camp – obviously the relics of a party of surveyors who, twenty years before, had set out across the lake and who had never returned. (These men, incidentally, were attached to an expedition led by Sir Vivian Fuchs, the British explorer who crossed Antarctica.) They knew where the hippopotamus browsed on the lake weeds, just as Count Teleki described them at the end of last century (though the elephants he saw have all since gone); and they were excellent naturalists. They pointed out to me a small black and white bird about the size of a pigeon whose body was mounted on two very long orange-coloured legs. This was the Stilt. The bird stands for such long periods in the shallows while it hunts for food that its legs become encrusted with salt. Then it flies off, and if you watch closely you will see that it trails its legs in the water so as to wash the salt away.

The salt in the water leaves its mark on every living thing around the lake. It stains the teeth and it turns the hair a shade of rusty brown or even white. One notices this particularly among the totos, the small Turkana boys who are forever in the water. However, when they shave their fuzzy heads (usually with a piece of broken glass) the hair comes up black again. McKay told me a pleasant anecdote of how on a visit to the city of Kampala, in Uganda, his hairdresser had remarked on the strange colour of his hair. 'That's what Rudolf does to you,' he told the man. There was a short constrained silence before the Commander realized that he was being misunderstood. He added hastily that he was not referring to a rival firm of hairdressers in the town but to the lake.

And clearly McKay and his wife loved the lake. They had discovered its rhythm and had become a part of it. Whenever they weary of their slowly revolving hot house existence they are always free to go off to a farm they own in the green hills outside Kitale, which is like visiting another planet. As for the Turkana themselves, who never go anywhere, who never look beyond the lake, or forward or backward in time, they seemed to me rather better off than most African tribes. Somewhere in his two large volumes Ludwig von Höhnel remarks, 'Though it is generally true that all negroes are but grown-up children, there is no real childhood in Africa.' There is some truth in this, for it is certainly a fact that in most primitive tribes the children hardly ever play; the boy is scarcely six or seven years old before he is sent off, spear in hand, to mind the cattle and the goats, and at the same age the little girl is already starting a lifetime's drudgery of drawing water, carrying loads, and preparing food.

Yet here on the lake the children did play, and there was a certain dignity about the adults which made them very far from childish. They were serious practical people. Without a doubt there are *longueurs* and miseries in their lives; an uninterrupted diet of fish can hardly be the ideal thing, and many of them are suffering from ailments which civilization could easily cure. But they did not seem to me to be basically discontented, not at any rate beyond Thoreau's notion that most people, anyway, live lives of quiet desperation. When we were ready to leave, the young men packed our baggage and rowed us back to the mainland. They wanted no payment. When I held out my hand to the leader of the group, a naked athlete of classical Grecian beauty, he came up smiling. He took my thumbs in his hand in the accustomed manner of the tribe; but then, fumbling like a girl who has made a slight *faux pas* at a party, but still smiling, he opened out his own pink palm and grasped mine in the strange amusing way of the white men's civilization. He felt a little awkward and uncomfortable in doing this, but it was very courteous.

CHAPTER NINE

THE NILE

MANY years have gone by since I first flew up the valley of the Upper Nile, starting the journey at Khartoum in the Sudan and ending it two thousand miles away at the source of the river in Uganda. Even then, in 1941, when planes did not fly nearly as high as they do today, there was not very much to be seen from the air except the endless desert and the meandering green line of the river, but there were frequent stops along the way, and these I remember just as distinctly as one remembers the islands on a long ocean voyage. Before we started we were held up for a day or two at Khartoum with engine trouble, and it was April, the hottest time of the year – so hot, in fact, that it was slightly painful just to touch the porcelain sides of your bath tub when you got up in the morning. A fearsome sandstorm known as a *haboob* was blowing, and it was only at the very end of the long torpid day that the town woke up at last.

Each morning, about an hour before the light began to fail, I used to walk down to the zoo with a book. Khartoum Zoo is quite unlike any other in the world. It lies on the left bank of the Blue Nile, just upstream from the point where the White Nile comes in from the southern Sudan, and it hardly covers more than two or three acres. The animals and the birds do not have that vacant and dispirited air that seems to overtake tropical creatures when they are transported to cold climates in the north; they were all born here in this hot-house atmosphere, and many of them are not kept in cages; they simply roam about in their natural state, grazing on the grass and the bushes or wading in the pond. At that hour there were hardly any visitors, and as I sat there reading the zebras, the antelopes, and many different kinds of long-legged birds used to gather round in a quiet and hesitating way that was something between curiosity and fear. It was very pleasant and very peaceful; it was also the more surprising one evening when I looked up from my book and found General de Gaulle standing before me. He was wearing a pale blue képi and a tropical uniform – the war was on and France had just fallen – and as I rose from my bench he saluted in a friendly informal way and went off to see the giraffes. Heaven knows what he was doing in that outlandish place. I only saw him twice more during the war; once at Casablanca with Roosevelt and Churchill, and then at the liberation of Paris, when he marched down the Champs-Élysées from the Arc de Triomphe at the head of his men and we were all in tears.

Yet it is not these two emotional moments that I recall when anyone now speaks of de Gaulle; it is this bucolic picture of the general among the flamingoes and the zebra in the Khartoum Zoo. And with the same isolated vividness I remember the rest of that journey : the quite staggeringly beautiful group of girls walking naked, with jugs on their heads, along the bank of the river, the warriors standing one-legged like storks and leaning on their spears among the conical grass huts at Malakal and Juba; the vast swamp of the Upper Nile which is known as the Sudd and which looks from the air like an enormous veined green leaf; and a thousand scrub-fires burning; and finally, on the shore of Lake Victoria itself, a waterfall which was then the beginning of the Nile's long passage to the sea. (The Nile, the Amazon, and the Missouri combined with the Lower Mississippi, are all around 4,000 miles long, and no two geographers seem to agree as to which of them is the world's greatest river.)

Such an experience creates a private myth in the mind; and also it was an accidental myth, since had I flown on another day in another aircraft that did not break down at Khartoum there might have been no sandstorm or scrub-fires, no General de Gaulle, no group of beautiful girls, and no crepuscular readings in the Khartoum Zoo. Moreover it was an experience that had a particular impact just then, since I was on my way from one campaign in the western desert of Egypt to another in Abyssinia, and all the future was intensely doubtful. This was time out from the war, and consequently the things that happened to me then were much romanticized in retrospect; I conceived that the river had a compelling and mysterious charm, that its inhabitants were a race of intense physical beauty living the true idyllic life, that pythons and other fabulous monsters rose out of its depths, that herds of elephants trumpeted in the swamps, and that everywhere tropical butterflies flew about. In short, it was all unspoiled and uncontaminated, savagery with a touch of grace.

Yet, myth or no myth, for seventeen years these notions were, for me, the Nile, and now in 1958 when I got back from Lake Rudolf it seemed to be no bad idea to discover just how true this picture actually was. I decided to return to Europe by way of the river, to follow its course from its beginnings in the lake to the beginning of my memory in Khartoum.

Not many people make this journey now, but there is nothing particularly difficult about it. You can buy a ticket anywhere. In a series of paddle-boats, trains, and cars you proceed downstream from the northern shore of Lake Victoria on the Equator on a regular and orderly course, and a fortnight later you find yourself in Khartoum.

When Sir Winston Churchill made this excursion in 1907 (he being then aged thirty-three and already the author of six books), he had recently become Under-Secretary of State for Colonies, and for much of the time he could think of nothing but of harnessing the river for electric power. 'The exit or overflow of the Great Lake,' he wrote, 'is closed by a natural rampart or ridge of black rock, broken or worn away in two main gaps to release the waters. Through these the Nile leaps at once into majestic being, and enters upon its course as a perfect river three hundred yards wide. Standing upon the reverse side of the wall of rock, one's eye may be almost on a plane with the shining levels of the Lake. At your feet, literally a yard away, a vast green slope of water races downward. Below are foaming rapids, fringed by splendid trees, and pools from which great fish leap continually in the sunlight. We must have spent three hours watching the waters and revolving plans to harness and bridge them. So much power running to waste, such a coign of vantage unoccupied, such a lever to control the natural forces of Africa ungripped, but vex and stimulate imagination. And what fun to make the immemorial Nile begin its journey by diving through a turbine!'

His wish has been granted, for the falls have since vanished and the source of the Nile is now a great concrete dam across which the main road from Kenya passes. It provides electric power for much of East Africa.

In Churchill's day there was no regular service for the first 500 miles of the journey downstream between the lake and Gondokoro in the southern Sudan (close to the modern Juba); however, he covered this distance in a matter of twenty days, partly by boat and partly on a bicycle – on which, incidentally, he made a good seven miles an hour along the jungle paths.

Nowadays you join the paddle-boat *Grant* at a place called Namasagali, about thirty miles below the lake. The *Grant* (which commemorates the name of Captain J. A. Grant who, with Captain J. H. Speke, discovered the source of the river in 1862) was built in 1924, and belongs to a more spacious age than this. She is a square-ended boat built on two decks, and has the appearance of a white shoe-box; not elegant but very comfortable. Like all the Nile steamers the *Grant* was brought out from England and up from the coast in parts and assembled on the river. Two wooden paddles thrash out the white water astern, and going down-stream you make perhaps six or seven miles an hour. Half a dozen cabins line the upper deck, and here the fittings run to brass and heavy mahogany. The bathrooms are labelled 'Western Type' and 'Eastern Type' (Indians, Africans, and coloured people generally falling under the latter category), and the water-filter is a homely up-ended stone jar made of some substance called 'leadless glaze'. Like most of the other gadgets of the vessel it is at least thirty years out of date and quite efficient. It bears the legend 'Pure drinking water is Life'. There is much space for the passengers to move about, and, as they sit on the upper deck watching the banks of the river sliding by, African servants in white robes, red cummerbunds, and turbans bring them drinks.

Down below the effects are less sumptuous. Half a dozen large barges, covering about a quarter of an acre, are lashed to the bows of the ship and are pushed ahead. Here the African passengers travel, together with their children, their goats, their chickens, their cooking fires, their branches of bananas, and their household goods. The African tribes who live at this end of the lake have a talent for colour – nothing but cotton cloth of the most hectic shades is considered suitable for women – and they form a sort of patchwork quilt as they lie about the decks of the barges in a close-packed mass with strong sunshine beating on them. Amid the breast-feeding of the babies, the crowing of the cocks, the bleating of the goats, the card-playing, the singing, and the cooking, the Mohammedan spreads his prayer-rug on the deck and prostrates himself towards Mecca. Many strange smells rise up, and it is rather as if you were travelling along with an eastern bazaar, a magic carpet that floats perpetually ahead on the surface of the river. One grows accustomed to it very quickly.

The white passengers in the upper deck were, I was informed by the crew, just about the usual thing: three nurses from Nairobi who were taking a few days' local leave to see the hippopotami and the crocodiles, a honeymoon couple, a Greek businessman bound for the Congo, and a young woman who vaguely, like myself, was 'seeing Africa'. There was also a lean, well-dressed Englishman who explained that after being incarcerated for forty years in an office in Europe he had retired three years before with enough money to see him through to the age of eighty-two – which he judged to be just about the limit of his expectation of life. Being without a family he used his London club as his home, or rather as a base, for he spent most of his time roaming round the world on a bicycle which he had specially built to accommodate his long legs. On the whole, he said, he enjoyed himself very much, though Africa had disappointed him; he was glad to be returning to Europe where he planned to spend the summer cycling through the Pyrenees.

All these people proposed to return to Uganda when we reached the Sudan border, while I alone was to continue on to Khartoum. It was nearly nightfall when, after a day's wait, we finally pushed out into midstream, and I was interested to know how the African helmsman could find his way in the dark, since there are no navigation lights along the river. 'He knows it,' the mate told me, 'by instinct. On the blackest night he can give you the position within 400 yards. Very rarely, in a thick fog or in a storm which is so bad the visibility is nil, we creep beside the bank or tie up, but for the most part we feel our way along the channels in midstream – and they keep changing with the wet and dry seasons. Just occasionally a hippopotamus breaks a rudder.'

We woke in the morning at Masindi Port, at the head of Lake Kyoga. Below this point the Nile breaks up into thirty miles of rapids which are unnavigable, and so we trooped ashore with our baggage for the second stage of the journey – an overland trip in a battered motor bus which was to take us to Lake Albert, some eighty miles away. Here we were to join another steamer, the *Robert Coryndon*.

I confess that up to this point the journey, though interesting, still fell a long way short of my myth of the Nile. The surrounding landscape was depressing; a dry hard scrub which seemed unable to cheer up though the rains had broken and a wild storm had poured down on us all through the night. The nurses had produced a portable radio that screeched and howled like a hunting hyena; others were complaining of the food (which can be best described as English boarding-house type, and except for breakfast is never one of the charms of Central Africa);

and the British globetrotter was hankering after his bicycle and the Pyrenees. Of the wild life – the pythons, the trumpeting elephants, and the butterflies – there was no sign whatsoever.

Then all at once, when we were half-way across to Lake Albert at Masindi Town, everything changed. The bus plunged into the country which astonished and enchanted the early explorers, and which started a craze for Central Africa in the sixties and the seventies of the last century. Flamboyants and purple jacaranda bloomed along the road. Among the trees in the rubber plantations bluebells were growing in a solid mass, and one might have imagined that one was in an English park in spring, except that on every other tree-trunk, about fifteen feet from the ground, a tropical tree-fern was sprouting; and here perched the colobus, the little black monkey with a snow-white stole around his neck. We ran on into plantations of pawpaw and coffee, where crowned cranes, which are almost as decorative as peacocks, paced about; and three baboons ran across the track. This was a stretch of genuine jungle. Everywhere green grass had sprung up overnight in the rain, the bottle-brush tree was flowering with a spiky crimson blossom.

Towards the end of the bus ride we had our first view of Lake Albert from the top of an escarpment where there is a hunting lodge used by the Duke of Windsor many years ago when, as the Prince of Wales, he came here on a shooting safari; and this is also a part of the eastern shore which the explorer Samuel Baker and his wife reached on 14 March 1864. Baker's feelings were a good deal stirred by the fact that he and his wife had taken several years to get here from Egypt, and that his were the first white man's eyes to survey the Lake. 'The 14th March,' he wrote in his diary. 'The sun had not risen when I was spurring my ox on after my guide who, having been promised a double handful of beads on arrival at the lake, had caught the enthusiasm of the moment. The day broke beautifully clear, and having crossed a deep valley between the hills, we toiled up the opposite slope. I hurried to the summit. The glory of our prize burst suddenly upon me! There, like a sea of quick-silver, lay far beneath the grand expanse of water – a boundless sea horizon to the south and south-west, glittering in the noonday sun; and on the west, at fifty or six miles distance, blue mountains rose from the bosom of the lake to a height of about 7,000 feet above its level. It is impossible to describe the triumph of that moment . . .'

Baker's ideas about the lake were of necessity somewhat sketchy; it was not nearly as big as he imagined (it is 100 miles long and about 20 miles wide, with an average depth of 40 feet), but he had indeed discovered a prize, for this is the second source of the Nile, and, with the green Congo hills and the Mountains of the Moon in the background, it is one of the spectacular sights of Central Africa.

We ourselves had arrived on just such a beautiful day as Bakes describes, for the clouds were now lifting, and we drove down to the shore in a burst of bright sunshine. Normally the lake maintains a flat calm, but today slate-green waves were breaking on the beaches. The *Robert Coryndon* turned out to be somewhat more sprightly than the *Grant*, and in the course of a single day she steamed to the head of the lake where the Nile comes in from the east and then flows out again to the north. All this country is ridden by the tsetse fly, and has been converted into a sanctuary for wild animals, the Murchison Park. Here one pauses for a day and transfers to yet another steamer, the *Lugard*.

We were now well on our way down the Nile, and were entering an area which, historically, is perhaps the most interesting part of Africa below the Sahara. For a hundred years at least, and probably for long before that, this corner of Uganda has been a battlefield and a point of rendezvous. There are no 'names' in this history, at any rate in its earlier stages, and no famous places to guide your eye on the map; the only records are the legends of the tribes and such evidence as the archaeologists and pre-historians can bring up from the earth. Yet it seems certain that, some-where about here in the unknown past, the Hamitic peoples, coming down from the north, collided with the Bantus, or true Negroes, coming up from the south and Central Africa; and that here eventually they fused to form a hybrid race, the Nilotes or the Nilohamites. For the most part they are tall, slender people, and in their facial appear-ance they tend more to resemble the early Egyptians than the negroes (or so it seemed to me on this journey). 'Physi-cally,' the late Professor Seligman wrote, 'the Nilotes show an aloofness and pride of race, with a lack of desire for European clothes or trade objects which is probably un-paralleled elsewhere in Africa.'

In the past fifty years a considerable library has been written about these people; the anthropologists have fallen on them with the avidity and persistence of explorers, classifying them into tribes, languages, and religions; and the eccentricities of their customs, in birth, marriage, and death, have been studied with microscopic care. But in the early part of last century not a single statistic existed, nothing was known; and the Arab traders then burst on this Shangri-La with frightful brutal force. Like the tribes themselves, some of the traders came from Egypt in the north and some from Zanzibar and the East African coast to the south. They met in the general vicinity of the Mur-chison Park and set up their slave camps there.

For some reason Arab traders don't qualify as explorers. Their names are hardly known, and if they left personal records of their adventures these have long since dis-appeared. All except the later men are submerged anony-mously in their own infamy. Yet the first traders were in the field long before Baker and the white missionaries, and a very profitable field it was. They wanted ivory and they wanted slaves, principally for the markets in Egypt, Tur-key, Arabia, and Persia, and in Central Africa they found both elephants and helpless human beings in abundance. They raided up and down the valley of the Upper Nile on the most rewarding big game hunt in African history; the tusks were loaded on to the backs of their captives, men, women, and children, and such of these as survived were either marched to the east coast for sale in Zanzibar or packed in barges and transported down the Nile to Khartoum. By the time the first white men arrived on the scene in the middle of last century, pillage, mass murder, and civil war were the common thing along the upper reaches of the river.

The explorers also arrived in two separate groups, men like Speke and Grant coming up from the south, and others like Baker travelling down from Egypt in the north; and once again this area was their point of meeting. Behind the explorers came the missionaries and foreign armies, and they were determined to bring western civilization to this dark blank spot on the map. But the Mohammedans were not ready to retreat as yet; Mohammed Ahmed Ibn Seyyid Abdullah, the son of a native schoolmaster, proclaimed himself a new Mahdi, a descendant of the prophet, and with an army of dervishes swept through the Sudan. In 1885 General Gordon, the British Governor-General, was killed in his palace in Khartoum, and for the next fourteen years the Mahdi controlled the valley of the Nile from the Egyptian border almost as far south as the Great Lakes in Central Africa, an area half as big as Europe. It was not until General Kitchener defeated the dervishes at the Battle of Omdurman in 1898 that civilization began to penetrate again, a civilization which, incidentally, the Nilotes had never cared for, not from what they had seen of it anyway. There was one further invader during these disturbances. This was the tsetse fly, which spreads disease and death among both human beings and domestic animals; and large areas which once were populated were now left barren.

So now, making one's way down the Nile from the Murchison Park, one sees on the banks of the river the relics of this short and agitated history; the site of an old slave camp and the crumbling earthworks of a fortress, the Christian mission stations and the mosques, the landmarks now overgrown with weeds which were once the pivot of a battle, and finally a deserted stretch of bank where the tsetse fly has put an end to all human ambitions, whether for good or evil.

But it is the people themselves, the survivors of so much monitory civilization, who chiefly catch your eye. We travelled at first through the country of the Madi tribe who live between the river and the Belgian Congo, and who by no means are to be confused with the Mahdi and the dervishes above, for they are pagans. Strictly speaking, they are not Nilotes at all, since their origins are in West Africa. You can see this very readily; they are less aggressive than the other riverine tribes, rather shorter in stature, and blessed with plump and cheerful good looks. They have taken rapidly to civilization in the past few years. Cotton is their chief crop, and now at this time of the year, in March, the harvest was just completed. At every sizeable village where we stopped they came swarming down to meet us on the bank, bringing their cotton with them to be transported to the ginnery, and this was an astonishing sight. Perhaps five hundred people would be waiting in a closely congested mass under the shade of the trees as we came round a bend in the river. Then, as we tied up, this mass would burst open and spill itself in a long ant-procession to the shore. The men wore shorts and the children ran naked. Such of the women who were clothed, the majority these days, wore a sort of toga wrapped around their torsos and tied above their breasts, and these togas were dyed in shades of shocking pink, bright yellow, and vermilion. On their backs the babies rode, papoose-like, in a sling, sometimes with a gourd or a pot like a storm-trooper's helmet clapped over their heads to keep the sun at bay. On their own heads (the hair cut extremely short and divided by perhaps half a dozen horizontal partings across the scalp) the women carried baskets of cotton and many different things: flat panniers of dried fish, trussed-up chickens, branches of bananas, tobacco leaves, bundles of firewood, water jugs, and sacks of grain.

On the shore the men helped their women to lift these

packages to the ground, and this was a moment of great animation, since some of the crowd were to join us as passengers in the ship (or rather on its attendant barges), others were coming ashore to meet their friends and relatives, and others again, their loads disposed of, slipped off their clothes and waded into the water to bathe. They did this with complete unselfconsciousness, and when they had bathed they drank the water and waded ashore again. The women's breasts were pendulous, but their backs were in the authentic Grecian mould and their wet black skin gleamed wonderfully in the sun. Young men kept arriving in dug-out canoes made of a single tree-trunk, and these they propelled with paddles that were shaped like a spade or a heart on a playing card. They stepped ashore bringing strings of fish in their hands. Everyone was cheerful. They kept shaking hands and greeting one another, and it was something more than a greeting; often one would see a couple reach out their hands to one another and stand there smiling, not precisely as lovers do, but simply enjoying the experience of being together. And presently one or the other would begin to dance, not moving the feet, but merely swaying their bodies and making a series of rhythmic gestures towards their partners with their shoulders and their arms. Under the trees a market had opened, the dried fish and the fruit spread out in the dust, and a beer shop was doing business. The beer was a seething white liquid in a tub, and the man in charge kept ladling it out to the customers with a gourd. At one place where an ancient motor bus stood waiting, a woman harangued the crowd with fierce, comic grimaces – perhaps she had had a little too much of the beer – and the people listened and laughed and urged her on. This was a village fair, a bazaar, a festival, a great day now that the crop was harvested and the boat had come in to take it away.

I found that I could spend hours together watching these scenes, sitting on deck with a pair of binoculars while the green banks glided by on either side, and, at the halts, wandering ashore among the bathers, the fishermen, the beer drinkers, and the dancers. There were curious glances, but no one seemed to mind a white man's presence, and it is clear that to this generation of the Madi the slave raids are not even a memory.

The river here, just above the Sudan border, is perhaps finer than it is ever to be again until it reaches the cataracts thousands of miles away in Egypt. There is a startling lushness in the landscape, and although the pattern keeps repeating itself – the papyrus reeds along the banks, the acacia trees and the green grass beyond, and in the distance the brown hills – nothing is re-stated exactly as it was before. This broken repetition, the constant change in sameness, makes it difficult to read a book; you keep glancing up for fear you have missed something. The Nile cabbage, the *pistia stratiotes*, is the real symbol of the river. It is a little plant of the liveliest and freshest green, about the size and shape of a full-blown rose, and it floats downstream on the moving surface of the water. The appearance of a single plant may never vary, but it joins with its neighbours in a thousand combinations, now in lines a hundred yards long, now in clusters, now in circles and curves that trace the currents and eddies in the stream. The Nile cabbage never fails; year after year it floats down with the endless persistence of the river itself.

As we got nearer to the Sudan border I began to notice that a more definite change was taking place; the cabbages were starting to group themselves into small drifting islands, and on these tall green grass was growing, the first warning of the great blockage of the Sudd that lay ahead. It was pleasant to watch these islands undulate in the waves of our wake, and often the sacred white ibises found a foothold there. They perched on the grass and rode the waves like bolls of white cotton swaying in the wind. Cranes and storks and many other birds came by, and in the evening the black darters, roosting in groups on the trees, spread out their wings to dry after a long day's fishing in the water. They had a vampire-ish look, like black bats or prehistoric pterodactyls.

It was not too hot except, unexpectedly, for an hour or two in the early evening, when one felt that one had had enough sunshine for the day. About four o'clock storm clouds would start to bank up at half a dozen places on the horizon, and presently, while the sunshine still poured down upon the river, these clouds turned black with falling rain. Short rainbows arched across from the dark into the blue. These weird lighting effects became intensified just before the sun went down, and then one saw chaotic reflections in the water that were closer to the theatre than anything in nature. They would be familiar to anyone who remembers Max Reinhardt's production of *A Midsummer Night's Dream*.

The captain of the *Lugard*, a young Englishman who had only recently joined the Nile service, asked me one day if I had ever read *Life on the Mississippi*. He thought it a fine book, very sound in all its practical details about the piloting of rivers, and he himself longed to go down the Mississippi one day so as to compare the hazards of the American stream with those along the Nile. Mark Twain's career as a river pilot was over even before the sources of the Nile were discovered, but his description of the Mississippi remains pretty true of the Upper Nile today. We had no gambling aboard the *Lugard*, but the cotton was here and so were the Negroes; and when we drifted into shallows a huge African with 'Uganda Marine' written across his jersey threw a line into the water to test the depth. When he called up to the bridge in Swahili his words, I imagine, might easily have been translated 'By the Mark One, By the Mark Twain . . .'

But there were differences too, the Captain explained; fire, not flood, was sometimes a danger on the Nile. Occasionally, he said, the vegetation rotting at the bottom of the swamps generated an immense heat and burst into flame on rising to the surface. The fires were apt to spread along the banks for a mile or more – the green papyrus was full of oil – and the dense acrid smoke made navigation impossible. Then there were the collisions with hippopotami, and the snakes that inhabited the floating islands – a particularly venomous species of snake, red on the back and white on the belly. Cannibals were still about, the Captain went on; we were actually approaching a point on the river where his crew was reluctant to go ashore.

I don't think the Captain believed in these cannibals any more than I did; still, it was pleasant to sit there in the evening light with a cool drink in hand making a world of terrors out of the green banks that drifted by on either side.

On the morning of the fifth day of the trip we woke to find the ship tied up, and, on an iron shanty on the shore, the green, blue, and yellow striped flag of the new Sudanese Republic was flying This was Nimule, the point where the Nile makes a sudden right-angled turn and breaks into cataracts for over a hundred miles. Here the *Lugard* turned round and bore away the nurses, the honeymoon couple, and the globe-trotting Englishman. I found, however, that I was not to continue alone into the Sudan, for we had now been joined by two women missionaries bound for Juba, and a gentle, grey-haired African preacher, the personification of Uncle Tom, who wore his reversed collar bravely in the heat. There was also a young white man from South Africa who had a refreshing notion of the world, namely that it was his to explore and enjoy for a while before he 'got stuck in an office'; and so he was wandering up through Africa to Europe with a rucksack on his back. Together we packed ourselves into a large touring car that was waiting and set off for Juba, the capital of the South Sudan, 120 miles away.

The less said about this drive the better. When Churchill got to Nimule in 1907 (a plaque on a tree now indicates where he camped for the night), he wrote '. . . somehow after Nimule the charm was broken . . .' One understood precisely what he meant. Up to this point you have been travelling through a semi-tropical water-garden where everything is clean and bright and fresh; now you take a sudden leap into another country and another way of life.

The mountains subside into hot and dusty plains of scrub. This is a landscape beaten down by the sun. Here the Mohammedans are master; the Swahili language is replaced by Arabic, and the feathered headdresses and the bright togas disappear. The people now wear the fez, the turban, and the galabieh, which looks like a nightgown and is nearly always plain white. In place of the illiterate Negroes with their deep voices, their white teeth, their natural grace, and their slowness there is now – at all events in the larger townships – a certain middle-eastern furtiveness, a whiff of sophistication. Colonel Nasser appeared to have a strong following even here in the far south of the Sudan, and his heavy confident features peered out at you from coloured oleographs in all the ramshackle shops along the street. Arabic music pours from the radio in the pavement cafés in a high-pitched whirling never-ending stream, and if you escape it in one place you are bound to be assaulted by it in the next. The customers, sitting on rush-bottomed chairs, closely scrutinize every stranger who passes by. The streets are unpaved and blowing with dust; the prevailing architecture is a galvanized iron shed. I looked for the grass huts that I remembered and they were there all right, but now they were surrounded by tall fences that blocked the view within, creating a kind of Moslem secrecy. Now, too, one realized that civilization means wastepaper. There was no paper in the primitive villages of the Upper Nile; here old arabic newspapers, discarded cigarette packets and other debris were constantly blowing about.

This, at any rate, was my first impression of Juba, which until this moment had occupied such a bright place in my myth of the Nile; and perhaps it was hardly fair. We had arrived there at the end of a four-hour drive through hot red dust at the hottest time of the day (squirming on the car seats, feeling our mouths dry up while our clothes grew wet with sweat); we were in a mood to see squalor and that in fact was what we saw. We trooped on board a dilapidated boat that was labelled quite simply 'Barge 3', and sat in a wired-in cage on the upper deck, to wait dispiritedly for tea. The shore was littered with junk and looked like an abandoned railway-yard. The heat was ferocious.

I admired the younger of the two missionaries, a nice girl, probably in her early twenties. She had been working in Nairobi in Kenya, which is a cool and cheerful place, and now she had been assigned to Juba for the next few years. They pointed out to her the ramshackle main street with its one hotel (the only hotel in the South Sudan), the mission, the church, the hospital, the place where she was to live, and she dropped a little as each new shed came into view; even the most devoted and experienced of missionaries must have done the same. But she revived somewhat when the tea arrived and managed to make a joke of it all. It seemed at the time to be a good deal more courageous than pious resignation, and it was quite clear that she would soon settle down in Juba and find virtues here that we others, as transients, would never see. Her companion, an older woman, had been on leave in the Kenya hills and was equally undismayed. 'I work with a small tribe of my own,' she told me, 'about a hundred miles from here.' I asked her where it was, and she answered, 'Oh, I don't know exactly where – I was never any good at places on a map.' She made a vague gesture towards the plains. 'It's out there somewhere.'

'How long have you been there?'

'Twenty years.'

'Alone?'

'Oh yes, I am by myself.' She explained that it was not lonely. She had set up a dispensary and had trained some of the young men as hospital dressers. She held her church services under the trees. She had planted a garden; and it was home.

While we were talking (we were all waiting on the barge to be cleared by the customs) the African preacher stood by, smiling continuously and looking more like Uncle Tom than ever. He was very nervous. Presently the pastor of the Mission arrived, a tall, good-looking man in freshly laundered shorts and shirt, and he welcomed his people in a

grave unenthusiastic way. 'Well, Eve. Good leave?' he said
to the lady who knew nothing about maps, and passed on
swiftly to the African preacher and the younger woman.
It was not unfriendly or exactly perfunctory; it was part of
the flatness and perhaps the emotional tiredness that de-
scends on people who live for many years in hot isolated
places and who are familiar with every detail of one another's lives, and who, especially in Africa, are committed
to an endless struggle in a primitive and reluctant world.

Clearly they had a thousand things to say to one another,
but all this would come out much later in a series of long,
slow conversations when they were alone. For the moment,
however, we were a polite and cosy party; the pastor
handed round the tea, inquiring if we took both milk and
sugar, and we might have been making a call at any vicar-
age anywhere except that a gang of Arab boys, the dead-
end kids of Juba, were running past and shouting rude com-
ments at us from the junk heap on the shore. We drank
our tea, and when the customs man had stamped their
passports the missionaries went off quietly together to their
huts and sheds in the town.

I had plenty of time to observe Barge 3 during the next
seven days. It was part of a cluster of other barges all
crammed with African passengers, and we were lashed to
a roaring, bell-clanging, chain-clashing, oil-smelling paddle-
boat which propelled us down the river like a mother duck
with her brood. It was Ramadan, the month when no
Mohammedan may eat or drink between dawn and sunset,
and the heat was intense. Throughout the day the crew
must have felt really wretched. They moved about with an
air of suppressed irritation and extreme lassitude, and it
was not the natural indolence of the Negroes; it was a
matter of sudden fits and starts and then long periods of
abstraction. A loud high-pitched shout would disturb the
afternoon siesta, and there would be a hideous rattling of
chains along the iron deck. Then all would subside into a
despairing silence broken only by the engine and the thrashing of the paddles. The men were extremely devout. (This

is something you notice more and more as you penetrate into the really primitive parts of the south Sudan – the more terrible the desert and the heat, the more poverty-stricken the people's lives, the more they tend to prostrate themselves in prayer, making twice or three times the required number of kneelings and bowings.) I used to watch the captain, who incidentally was not called the captain, but the engineer, apparently a higher title on the river. He was a lean handsome man wearing a galabieh and a lace skullcap, and he sat cross-legged on a shelf on the bridge directing operations. Every few hours he descended to the deck below, and there he spread out a little doeskin prayer-rug and prostrated himself, shifting his position when we rounded a bend so that he continued to face towards Mecca. Someone had tethered a baby gazelle at the place where he prayed, and it bleated continuously on one high note that easily penetrated the general uproar of crowing cocks, of baa-ing goats and the crashing of the engine. The engineer remained for the required time in a trance of worship, and then, rolling up his doeskin and placing it under his arm, made his way slowly back to the bridge.

Apart from the South African and another young man, a bearded Englishman who was also wandering around the world – he had already crossed India and Central Africa by himself in a Land Rover – and myself, there were no other white men on board, where, a year or two ago, before the British left the Sudan, there would have been a dozen or more, some of them changing for dinner. On Barge 3 most of the other passengers were Mohammedans who rarely left their cabins. The women in particular sat or lay on their bunks all day and all night, apparently unaffected by the heat. They did not pray or observe the fast; their servants kept padding bare-footed along the deck bringing them little bowls of rice and baskets of mangoes. They threw the mango skins out of the cabin doors while they ate.

We others meanwhile drifted into a lackadaisical routine and no day had any definite beginning or ending. 'Time vanishes,' Churchill wrote when he made this journey, 'and nothing is left but space and sunlight.' It would be useless to pretend that it was not monotonous. One woke at dawn, sweating under the electric fan that seemed to do nothing more than move the stale air in circles round the cabin. One punctuated the day with drinks, with meals, with repeated lukewarm showers, and with hours of reading; and although looking back I can see that this slow passage gave a sort of depth and frame to one's impressions, one was not conscious of this at the time. Most of the day we sat in the wired-in compound on the forward deck, and it was like being confined to one's room with a vague indefinite illness which was not painful or unpleasant but slightly narcotic in its effects.

In these circumstances one reads books in quite a different way. Not only do you make a re-appraisal of them, so that those which before seemed good now sometimes seem trivial; inevitably the actual experiences that happen to you on your journey get mixed up with the book you chance to have before you at the moment. And the results are often bizarre. One year, for example, when I was travelling through Tanganyika I was doing a good deal of reading about the Russian revolution in 1917, and it was an odd thing to look up from Trotsky or the collected letters of Lenin and see, only a few yards away, a group of lions watching me from the long grass; or perhaps meet the eye of some great gaunt bird like the marabou, which in its own way could be as grave and relentless as Lenin himself. Earlier that same year, when I had been on the Abyssinian border, I had read *Emma* and *Pride and Prejudice*, and they went well. It is the contrast, of course, that startles you. There may be no possible connexion between Mr Darcy's privileged, mannered world of eighteenth-century England and a naked African flaying a dead warthog beside the track, but when such odd coincidences do occur they have a certain theatrical charm. All Russian novelists are good for African travel. Earlier on this present trip I read *The Idiot* and Tolstoy's *The Cossacks* in the Rift Valley, and now on the Nile I found that the latest volume of the Boswell papers – *Boswell in Search of a Wife* – passed the time very agreeably. Really light reading for some reason does not do in Africa, and detective stories and mysteries (with the possible exception of Chesterton's *Father Brown*) are definitely bad. Books about Africa itself, preferably written by the explorers and illustrated with plenty of nineteenth-century engravings and maps, are probably the best reading, but travel books about other places are apt to seem irrelevant and purposeless, if not downright boring. In the end Jane Austen may be the most rewarding.

Below Juba the Nile makes a great swoop to the northeast through low but fairly fertile banks. This is the territory of the Dinka tribe, and here almost immediately you cast off the Arab influence and the sophistication of the Moslems. It is more primitive than the Madi country; indeed, it is one of the least civilized parts of the whole continent. There are about a million Dinkas, and upon any count they are some of the most interesting people in Africa. In its study of the Nilotes the International African Institute says that the Dinkas 'consider their country the best in the world and everyone inferior to themselves'. They have resisted interference from outside probably more fiercely than any other tribe. According to the Institute, touchiness, pride, and reckless disobedience is their customary reaction towards authority. The Dinkas are conservative and serious people; they believe strongly in the rights of the individual. Nature certainly has helped them to maintain this aggressive attitude, for they are probably the tallest people in the world on the average (many are six foot five or more) and are proportionately tough. But they are not muscular; both men and women have slight lithe figures, narrow hips, and extraordinarily long legs. Their hair is frizzy and their complexion dark brown verging on black. Some have broad noses, but most I saw had aquiline features, thin lips, and long finely-shaped noses. They resolutely refuse for the most part to wear any clothes at all beyond a small apron or a few strings hanging from a leather girdle, but even these are often discarded. However, they like jewellery, especially when they are young, and they scar their faces and bodies with cicatrices. Often you will see a man who has decorated himself by covering his entire body with grey ash. It gives him a macabre and ghostly appearance, but he is always a commanding sight with his long spear and his direct and challenging glance. The Dinka is a cattle breeder, and he dotes on his animals. A boy on being given a bull by his father will grow up with the beast, living with it day and night, calling it by an endearing name and singing it songs to keep it happy while it grazes in the fields. It is impossible not to like these proud and truculent people.

For preference the Dinkas would live on milk and blood, and nothing else but hunger drives them to scratch the surface of the dry soil and grow a little millet. Just now, when the Nile was at its lowest at the end of the dry season, they were gathered everywhere around the waterholes spearing and netting fish. It was a primitive business, the simple casting of a weighted hand net and repeated jabbings with their spears into the mud; but they were hauling in the fish by the hundredweight and these were left stinking in the sunshine until they were ready to be eaten.

Nothing of my seventeen-year-old memory of the beauty of these people was false. They came wading into the river as we went by, and crowded around us at the stopping places; and they were as graceful and elegant as herons. They lifted up their hands towards us with open palms, not asking for anything but as if to say, 'Well, there you are, a passing spectacle on the river.' But they hated being photographed, not, I think, out of any modesty for their nakedness, but probably because they regard the camera as an evil eye which threatens and interferes with their privacy – which of course it does. It takes away from them an image, a likeness, which they feel ought not to be exposed to strangers and possibly enemies. When the young Englishman with the beard was photographing from the deck one day a six-foot warrior came rushing towards him across a sandbank and into the water in a perfect frenzy of rage. He pointed his finger at us, and then raising his spear, made a series of vicious upper-cuts into the empty air; it was obvious that he would have disembowelled my young friend there and then if he could have reached him. On another day both the men and the women began hurling stones and bits of mud when the camera appeared, and one of our fellow passengers, a northern Sudanese in a city suit, an educated man, came up and asked if we had permission to take pictures. He was in his own way almost as angry as the tribesman on the shore, but for an altogether different reason : he hated the idea of these 'backward' villages being photographed. The nakedness of their inhabitants was to him an immodest and shameful thing, and to take pictures of them was to give a false impression of the Sudan. This was bad propaganda. The world, he thought, should know about the new republic the Sudanese were trying to build up – the schools, the hospitals, the western clothes, the tractors, and the hydraulic projects; soon in any case all this primitiveness in the south would be swept away. He was right, one supposes, and we stopped photographing after this.

Still, it was pleasant to have this last glimpse of simplicity. I liked the Dinka villages much more than Juba. They looked like Red Indian encampments of a century or two ago : tall teepees made of grass and arranged in a rough circle on the bank, covering about an acre. Fires burned on the ground before the huts, and in the background the white huge-horned cattle of the tribe grazed. There was great activity everywhere, the men paddling about in canoes made of hollowed-out tree trunks, the women coming down to the river with water jugs on their heads precisely as I remembered them; and the children were especially charming, not pot-bellied or spindly like the children of the other tribes further up the river, but lithe and graceful and firm-breasted; and that, one could see from their parents, was the way they were destined to continue to be even in late middle-age.

It was a pity, of course, that so many of the girls had

plastered their shaven pates with reddish grease, and had worked their hair into thick strands like a mop; and many of them were already taking to rust-coloured cloaks that reached to the knees. But the chokers of red beads around their necks were very gay, and when they smiled their gleaming white teeth split their round cannon-ball heads into two; it was a whale of a smile.

Altogether these villages throw out an impression of a calm and coherent way of life. Usually each village or group of villages is autonomous, and has its 'Spear-Chief' and its elders who administer the ancient laws (some of which are odd but perfectly understandable, such as the rule that every man must wear a small apron when his mother-in-law is present). All the tribe, as a community, acknowledge 'Jok', who is the 'Sky-God', the remote and supreme ancestor, the universal spirit, the source of the mystic force of life.

From Jok comes the rain which continues on and off from April until November. As the Nile rises in flood the Dinkas retreat with their cattle to higher ground. In the dry season from November to April they return to the banks of the river, and they rebuild such of their huts as have been eaten by termites or swept away; these were the villages we were seeing now. Light rainstorms swept the river in the early evenings as we went along, and already in these last days of March there were signs that the tribes would soon be on the move again. We saw little wild game, just an occasional hippopotamus bobbing up out of the brown water, the odd crocodile slithering off the bank, a few waterbuck, and once or twice small groups of elephant browsing among the reeds, the last survivors of the great ivory-trade slaughter of eighty or ninety years ago.

On the third day out from Juba we hit the Sudd. The word hit is precise. Channels have been cut through this fantastic swamp, but they are narrow, with many bends, and our square cluster of barges was an unwieldly lump, not at all designed for cornering. We lurched erratically from side to side, hitting first one bank and then the other with a soft but heavy thump. Often for ten minutes at a time we would go into reverse and then edge forward again, scraping along the low cliffs where the current races, tearing away great chunks of earth and papyrus reeds, before we got around a corner. At times we floated helplessly sideways until we crashed into a sandbank. Now the bell in the engine room was never silent, and although the engineer appeared quite unmoved, sitting cross-legged up there on the bridge, the rest of us found it an exacting experience, rather like riding a bucking horse. So now, for the next three days we went lurching, swaying, lunging, and bumping down the river, nothing to see on either side but an endless feathery avenue of papyrus. It stretched away like a green ocean, and the horizon was a perfect circle under a hot white sky.

Samuel Baker gives a fine idea of what the Sudd was like when he first saw it in 1870, the stream being then completely blocked. He says: 'The immense number of floating islands that were constantly passing down the stream of the White Nile had no exit; thus they were sucked under the original obstruction by the force of the stream, which passed through some mysterious channel until the subterranean passage became choked with a wondrous accumulation of vegetable matter. The entire river became a marsh, through which, by the great pressure of the water, the stream oozed through innumerable small channels. In fact, the White Nile had disappeared.'

This was the obstacle which for 2,000 years at least blocked every attempt of the explorers to get to the source of the river. Two centurions sent by the Explorer Nero were forced to turn back, and from that time to the nineteenth century numberless unsuccessful expeditions set out. The mystery of the Nile intrigued civilization then even more than outer space does today. Baker managed to cut a way through only to find that the mass of weed closed up behind him. In 1874 an Egyptian expedition opened up a channel, but within four years it was choked again. Once more in 1880 the Egyptians cut a way through, but soon after that the dervish rebellion put an end to any further clearance for the next fourteen years. It was not until the early years of this century that the British succeeded in making a permanent channel; a group of engineers under a Major Malcolm Peake did this by cutting out huge blocks of vegetation – some of them a mile long and twenty feet thick. These segments were then divided into blocks each ten feet square, and these were hauled out bodily from the river by gun-boats working with wire hawsers downstream from the blockage; a hot and trying job that took four years.

The Sudd continues for about 250 miles, nearly half the length of Italy. Were it ever drained – and the project has been discussed – it could become another plain of Lombardy, though much larger and probably quite as rich. At present, however, it is almost without life, a vast pitiless desolation that seems, as you pass through, to be more terrible than a desert, for it has none of the desert's antiseptic properties or its clear light. This swamp is hostile and primeval, something out of the unformed beginning of the world. The papyrus itself is rather a beautiful plant that grows to above twelve feet in height on a long, green, cane-like stalk, and then spreads out in a foliage of delicate fans. But when it is seen like this, *en masse*, in a mad abundance that goes on mile after mile, day after day, it is oppressive, claustrophobic, even a little sinister.

One day when we were tied up for an hour or two mending a broken rudder I went ashore, and within a few yards of the bank found myself completely surrounded by walls of exactly identical stalks. It required only a few steps to get myself back to the river, but the mind creates nightmares in this wilderness, and it was all too easy to imagine that the boat had sailed without me, that I was utterly abandoned and certainly doomed to die. Visions of pythons – those cherished pythons of my myth of the Nile – rose up from the swamp to crunch me. Barge 3, when I got back, seemed to me then like a suite at the Ritz.

Yet the fires in the Sudd are very beautiful, and they

were all round us now, day and night, crackling and snarling, sending up great columns of smoke into the sky. One sees them on the horizon ahead some five or ten miles away, but an hour or more may go by on the winding river before you draw level with the flames, and then the heat comes out and strikes you from the shore. In the darkness sometimes it looks as if a ring of distant cities is on fire, and the smoke is lit from below with a lurid pinkish-purplish light, an effect that for some reason used to remind me of historical paintings, Napoleon's retreat from Moscow, perhaps, or the last days of Pompeii. Then in the morning you see the wreckage on the bank. The papyrus stalks lie twisted and tangled on the blackened earth like the girders of some great building that has burned down in the night, and there is an acrid smell in the air.

The fires attract the small birds along the river. You see them darting into the very edge of the flames to snatch the insects driven out by the heat. These birds, like the Sudd itself, exist in an impossible profusion. I thought they were locusts when I saw them first – they made a kind of brown stain across the sky – and it was only through binoculars that I made out the shapes of tiny feathered wings, millions upon millions of them. They flew at great speed and in a dense mass, weaving and wheeling together in the air, constantly changing direction, and like bats they must have some sort of radar to guide them, for they never collide.

The Nile cabbages vanish in the Sudd – perhaps they are broken up by the rapids above Juba – but they are replaced by the water hyacinth, which is even more prolific. It is a green fleshy creeper with a pale purple flower, and it reaches out, floating, from the bank. Long filaments of the plant constantly break away and sail off down the river. We kept smashing into these green rafts, and although they were torn to pieces by the paddles they always gathered themselves together again in our wake.

Outcrops of hard land occur at intervals in the Sudd, and here a tree or two will grow and a village will spring up. We were now entering the territory of the Nuers, a kindred tribe to the Dinkas, but the people are shorter and less hand-some. Many of the men and the younger girls were quite naked except that they wore tight coils of steel wire round their upper arms, and these made the flesh below bulge horribly like tubers. Some sported an ornament that was new to me on the Nile: a string of little metal balls tied round the posterior in such a way that they tingled pleas-antly as the wearer walked along. It seemed to give the girls a good deal of simple pleasure. Almost all of them too had shaven their bullet heads, leaving only a small top-knot on the pate. The shaven part of the skull was ringed with cicatrices in parallel lines.

This custom of self-mutilation grows more and more pro-nounced as you descend the Nile. One is assured by the anthropologists that there is always a reason for the scars; that they are a matter of tribal convention, or of religion, of adornment or of initiation ceremonial, or of sex. The desire to mutilate the body is said to be one of the first in-stincts of primitive people. Yet the custom is still difficult to understand, even when you are confronted with it like this in every village you pass by. You see many tribesmen with their incisor teeth knocked out, but neither they nor anyone else can tell you why they do it.* Certainly no animal prac-tises self-mutilation, and animals presumably are more primitive than human beings. Nor could I ever see that cicatrization was attractive, let alone beautiful. One or two of the African women on our boat were quite horribly scarred – great inch-wide gashes down their cheeks – and now we began to encounter young men who had managed to raise a series of pustules as big as grapes across their foreheads. In order to achieve these malformations they must have made deep cuts with a knife and have rubbed some irritating juice into the wounds. They looked quite terrible. Moreover, the repellent effect is doubled when you encounter these scars on a man who has been educated somewhat and who wears ordinary western clothes. He

* There is a theory that, with these teeth removed, a patient suffering from lock-jaw can be fed.

aspires to be civilized and indeed he often is; yet he remains in appearance an outlandish savage.

The Nuers seemed to me to be a poorer race than the Dinkas, and their poverty increased steadily as we went deeper and deeper into the Sudd. In the first Nuer villages we passed, the people had a definite knowledge of money; the men who came on board to unload cargo from the barges were naked, but they lined up afterwards to get their pay. At another place where we had anchored at midnight under the strong beam of a searchlight a warrior tried to sell me a dead crocodile. Elsewhere the villagers who specialized in the making of straw mats came thronging down to the shore to sell their products to the passengers. They made a strange sight standing there on the bank, every man, woman, and child clutching a twelve-foot roll of matting, and they held out their hands for payment in a modest pleading sort of way. But now the Sudd closed in more relentlessly than ever. The villages grew further and further apart and finally degenerated into single homesteads of crude grass huts. On all but the river side they were hemmed in by the papyrus. Clearly they were hungry. I saw one group of men flaying a dead crocodile, which can hardly be a palatable diet, and everywhere the people were pitifully thin and listless. Once we passed a small herd of elephant rooting about in the reeds quite close to a group of huts, but the tribesmen had obviously made no attempt to attack them; and indeed the people looked hardly strong enough to embark on such an enterprise.

It was interesting to watch their reactions to our boat. It made quite a commotion on the river and was certainly the most imposing object for many miles around. In the more highly developed settlements upstream it was a great centre of interest. But here we did not attract much attention. The men and women sitting outside their huts hardly bothered to look up, and some elaborately turned their backs. It could hardly have been boredom that made them behave in this way, for the fortnightly passage of the boat was a big event on the river. The more probable explanation seems to be that these people did not like to be confused by strange objects or jerked out of the narrow uneventful rhythm of their lives, any more than we ourselves, perhaps, when fishing in a stream or rigging a boat, would wish to be confronted by a roaring express train or a jet plane going by. We too might not look up. And so one presumes that our arrival, having no purpose or meaning in the villagers' lives, was nothing more than an intrusion and an interruption. They were absorbed in their own dullness.

I recall one incident of really desperate sadness. Looking up from my book one day (a P. G. Wodehouse novel, alas, not very amusing in these surroundings), I saw a single solitary boy sitting in the shade of a lean-to shelter on the bank. He did not stir or make any sign. This was strange, for even here the piccaninnies usually waved and called to us, and normally they ran in packs. Then, looking closer, I saw that this boy's stomach was enormously swollen by some disease. He was obviously in a deep daze of pain and apathy; nothing could amuse him or enlist his attention any more. One is particularly unwise in Africa to jump to conclusions, yet it could be that the boy had been segregated from the rest of his family and had been left alone there in the shelter to die. I watched him until we turned a corner but still he never moved.

By now we had been almost three days in the Sudd, and were approaching Lake No, where a tributary called the Bahr El Ghazal joins the main stream. Here the river makes a sharp turn to the east, and almost at once there were many signs that at last we were leaving the Sudd behind us. We were still a long way as yet from Luxor and the great riverside temples of ancient Egypt – they lay another thousand miles downstream beyond Khartoum – still we were returning to civilization of a sort. Wide dusty plains replaced the papyrus, and thousands of cattle were grazing there. The villages were dreary and semi-sophisticated places with galvanized iron sheds along the banks and broken-down motor-buses standing about; more and more of the inhabitants wore clothes. Surprisingly, the wild life increased; flocks of Abdim's storks rose from the reeds and it was a common thing to see crocodiles sunning themselves on the sandbanks, and groups of snorting hippopotami rising to the surface. Further off I caught sight of antelopes which may have been those which are peculiar to the Sudan, and which are known by the splendid name of Mrs Gray's Lechwe. The continual bumping of the boat into the banks came to a blessed end at last; the river now ran broad and straight towards the east. There were many fishermen paddling about in vee-shaped rafts made of dried reeds tied together, and once again we saw hills in the distance.

There was a sudden uproar in the night just before we reached Malakal. We ran down a fishing boat in the darkness, and in a hullaballoo of shouting three scared and bewildered young men were hauled on board. I came on them in the morning crouching on the deck beside the engine. Heaven knows why they should have been put in that horrible place; the stench of hot oil was overpowering and the noise was such that it was impossible to speak. Obviously this was the first time these youths had come so close to civilization. They had been plucked straight out of their antediluvian world by this threshing monster on the river, and now they were utterly confused. They squatted there, black and naked, just a string of wire around their waists, their faces heavily scarred above the eyebrows, and their eyes were like those of trapped animals. At Malakal police came on board to take charge of them, very smart police in khaki with a blue felt hat turned up on one side. They kept asking questions, and the three young fishermen gazed up at them trying desperately to understand. All they wanted to say, no doubt, was that they had lost their boat and now they wanted to go home. But here at Malakal we were back again in the world of law courts, witnesses, and statements. When I went ashore the head policeman had produced a notebook.

Malakal (population 6,800) is another Juba, except that it is somewhat larger, busier, and dustier. It has, however,

one distinction and it is important: this is the territory of
the Shilluks and close by on the river at Fashoda is the
dwelling place of the divine king of the tribe. When Frazer
published his tremendous work, *The Golden Bough*, in 1890,
very little was known of the tribal customs of Central and
East Africa. Frazer was mainly concerned to explain the
significance of the prehistoric King of the Wood in the
sacred grove of Diana on Lake Nemi, in the Alban Hills just
south of Rome. But he had a moment of prescience when
he wrote his preface to the abridged edition of his twelve
volumes: 'How far the facts point to an early influence of
Africa on Italy, or even to the existence of an African
population in Southern Europe, I do not presume to say.
The prehistoric relations between the two continents are
still obscure and still under investigation.' This is akin to
Darwin's contention that the first human beings to inhabit
the earth lived in Africa, and it is fascinating, now that
we know a good deal about the divine kings of the Shilluks,
to read the famous opening passage of *The Golden Bough*.
Describing the sanctuary on Lake Nemi, Frazer says: 'In
this sacred grove there grew a certain tree round which at
any time of the day, and probably far into the night, a grim
figure might be seen to prowl. In his hand he carried a
drawn sword, and he kept peering warily about him as if at
every instant he expected to be set upon by a murderer;
for the man for whom he looked was sooner or later to
murder him and hold the priesthood in his stead. Such was
the rule of the sanctuary. A candidate for the priesthood
could only succeed to office by slaying the priest, and having slain him, he retained office till he was himself slain by
a stronger or craftier. The post which he held by this pre-
carious tenure carried with it the title of king; but surely no
crowned head ever lay uneasier, or was visited by more
evil dreams, than his. For year in and year out, in summer
and winter, in fair weather and in foul, he had to keep his
lonely watch, and whenever he snatched a troubled
slumber it was at the peril of his life. The least relaxation
of his vigilance, the smallest abatement of his strength of

limb or skill of fence, put him in jeopardy; grey hairs might seal his death-warrant.'

And he adds: 'No one will deny that such a custom savours of a barbarous age, and, surviving into imperial times, stands out in striking isolation from the polished society of the day, like a primeval rock rising from a smooth-shaven lawn.'

When Frazer was writing this the actual embodiment of his divine murderer-king was living at Fashoda, and in fact his successors still reside there to this day.

'According to Shilluck folk-lore,' says Seligman, an authority on the subject, 'there was once a period when any man of the royal family who could slay the king might reign in his stead, and this is given as the origin of the still existing practice that the king sleeps by day and is awake at night, for it was only at night, when alone or with his women, that his life might have been attempted with hope of success. The Shilluk tell of grim fights round the huts of the royal wives, neither the king nor his assailant calling for assistance, for it was said to be a point of honour for the matter to be settled in single combat.'

In more recent times there were some refinements of this custom; the Shilluk king was simply strangled or walled up in a hut and allowed to die. Nowadays, under tribal law, the king can still be killed by a rival claimant to the throne, provided the claimant is of royal blood, and for this reason none of the king's sons or the sons of other previous kings are allowed near Fashoda at night.

The Shilluks, however, did not murder their king for sport, or because some rival was strong enough to seize power; they had a much more practical reason. They believe that their king is inspired with divine power: he is a rain-maker, a spell-binder, a bestower of fertility and health. They also believe that their own destiny as a race is entirely bound up with the physical condition of the king; if he is healthy and strong so are they all, and the crops will flourish. If on the other hand he is weak and ailing, then the whole tribe, about 100,000 of them, will suffer too. Consequently, when the king's powers diminish he must be quickly killed to make way for a healthier man; to allow him to die naturally might mean that the whole tribe too might die. To quote Seligman again: '... it was in order that the spirit [of the race] might be housed in a thoroughly healthy body that the habitual practice of the Shilluk was to slay their king directly he showed signs of ill-health or even of such gradual senescence as was evidenced by his inability to satisfy his large number of wives.'

Among the Dinkas who also have divine kings (though in a much more restricted way) it has even been the practice for a declining ruler to accept the inevitable and accomplish his own end; one method was for the unhappy man to deposit himself in an open grave, and then, having imparted his last words of wisdom to the tribe, he would give the order for the grave to be filled in.

All these practices are now on the decline. Yet it is impossible to make this journey down the Nile without feeling that deep mysteriousness still remains. After all, the majority of these people are still pagans, they are beset by strong instincts and secret dreams, and to be with them is to feel very close to the beginning of things. When one is told, as I have been told at least a dozen times in Africa, of some case in which a man wills himself to death because he believes himself to be under a curse, it is unwise to dismiss the story as ridiculous. Very often the man does die. He succumbs to a fatalism that is beyond all western reason. There exists too a pervading sense of rootlessness, of impermanence, almost of fragility, in these people's lives. It is a part of the Tahitian islanders' cry in the Gauguin paintings: 'Who am I? Where do I come from? Where am I going?' Sonia Cole in her *Pre-history of East Africa* says, 'After stone age times the cultural stagnation of most of Africa south of the Sahara set in. Here was no Bronze Age, and the Iron Age penetrated southwards and into the interior of the continent very slowly and gradually.' These Nilotic tribes in particular were driven southwards because of the 'progressive desiccation' of the Sudan over the last

6,000 years. But 'we know very little of the origin of most of the present East African tribes,' Miss Cole goes on, 'whence they came and when, or why they were so uninterested in material comforts, labour-saving inventions, and cultural and artistic productions. We are almost entirely dependent on oral tradition for the interpretation of their past history . . .'

It is clearly a history which goes back a very long way, at least as far and perhaps further than the divine kings in the sacred grove of Nemi in Italy. It is also a history in which, until recent years, there has been no real progression; as with the Nile itself it has continued to be ever-changing and yet always the same. The Nilotes still rise like Frazer's primeval rock from the smooth-shaven lawn of modern civilization.

We were now nearing the end of our journey, and although we were still nearly two thousand miles away from the mouth of the river in the Mediterranean, it was in a way like leaving Africa itself. Now the huts were more like houses and very neatly and strongly built. A road ran beside the river, and one saw an occasional lorry driving along it through the dust. Still the small birds streamed in billions along the bank, and once I saw a group of tribesmen cutting up a young hippopotamus which they had speared among the reeds. But now there were other steamers paddling by, and the atmosphere was that of a great estuary which presently would lead on to wharves and docks and advertising signs. In point of fact the river does nothing of the sort; it plunges into drier and drier desert. Beyond the green fringe of the banks there is a wilderness of sand which is even more desolate than the Sudd. It may be less claustrophobic than the great maze of papyrus upstream, but there is something forbidding in this extremity of emptiness and at times the heat – a dry heat now – is beyond all bearing. There is a quality of harshness and sluggishness in the atmosphere which is very strange. The fish eagle had been our constant companion all the way from the Equator, even as constant as the egret and the hippopotamus, and it had been a wonderful thing to see the rapidity with which he launched himself from a bough to snatch a fish from the river. But here on the edge of the desert even this swift marauder seemed to be affected by the general inertia.

One afternoon, when I was watching one perched on a bare thorn, there was an astonishing incident. Three or four large fish – they looked like *Tilapia* – rushed clean out of the water on to a sandbank, and they were immediately followed by a young crocodile, his jaws snapping furiously. The fish made a last frantic effort and wriggled back into the water, and although one of them vanished in a quick crunch of the crocodile's jaws the others got away. All this happened within twenty yards of the fish eagle, and there was ample time for him to have got his share of the spoils – no eagle on the Upper Nile would have missed a chance like that – but the whole affair was over before this bird spread his wings. He hovered about disconsolately for a while before he returned to his perch, and he was like one of those fat urbanized seagulls that have grown slow with too much gorging in the wake of ocean steamers.

At Kosti, which is about 200 miles from Khartoum, one leaves the river once more, and here you join a train for the last lap of the journey. I cannot say that I saw the last of Barge 3 with much regret, and yet I am astonished at the clarity with which I can recall the slightest detail about her: the engineer praying beside the crying gazelle, the broken streamers of hyacinths and papyrus fronds hanging in festoons along our sides, the churning of the electric fan all night, the smell of the river, and the taste of the sweet gritty grounds in the little cups of Turkish coffee that were served on board; if these things had been really unpleasant no doubt I would have blocked them out of my memory. As things are, they form a quite isolated and distinct experience which came to an abrupt and definite end with my arrival at Khartoum.

I had a day and a half in Khartoum before I joined a plane to Europe, and that was time enough to discover that although it had grown to a city of some 90,000 people while

I had been away, it too had changed only to remain the same. No *haboob* was blowing, but on this day in early April (as in that other April seventeen years ago) the temperature rose to 110 degrees, and at the confluence of the White and the Blue Niles one could still see the two rivers running side by side, the one brownish-white and the other greyish-blue. On the left bank you could still go over the ground where Churchill, as a young subaltern, charged with the 21st Lancers in the Battle of Omdurman in 1898; and Kitchener, the British General in command, still looks very fine in bronze riding his horse 'Diplomat' in a green square on the opposite bank of the river.* In the Palace, which is a splendid white pile such as you might see beside the Thames in London were it not for the Moorish flourishes, you could still examine the cannon and the breastplates captured from the dervishes at Omdurman; some of them are said to have been presented to the local inhabitants by Napoleon when he made his conquest of Egypt. In the courtyard is the curving flight of steps upon which General Gordon was assassinated.

If you walk southwards from the Palace you will obtain a pretty good idea of the city, a cross-section, as it were, of its history and of its present aspect. At first you see the feluccas, with their mutton-chop sails, which have been sailing on the river since the time of the Pharoahs, then the official town built among trees by Kitchener sixty years ago (the streets laid out in the form of the Union Jack), then the mosques, the bazaars, and the modern city buildings, then the railway yards, and finally the desert. All this was very much as I remembered it.

In the evening I went down to the zoo. Here there was even less change. No General de Gaulle, of course (at that moment he was preparing to make yet another march down the Champs-Élysées), but the leopards, the zebras, and the gazelles were there. In the twilight I found my old seat beside the pond, and presently the animals began to gather round. I looked for the long-legged storks and the marabou

* In recent months the statue has been removed.

and the shoebill, which is a bird with a head like a boot and a steady, exasperated stare. They were all there. One of the shoebills took up a position about six feet away and glared at me fixedly, almost as though he recognized me and was not much enjoying the experience. He was a mournful bird. He was as old as a primeval rock.

London–Rome, 1956–9

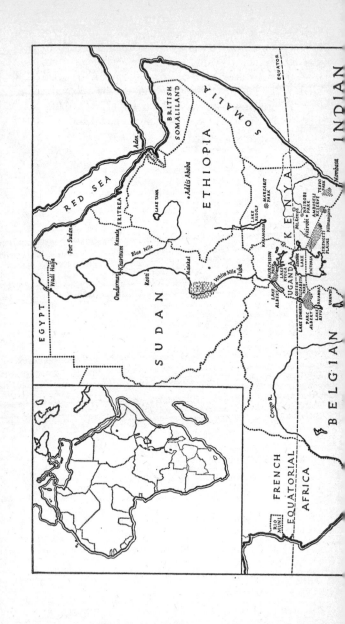

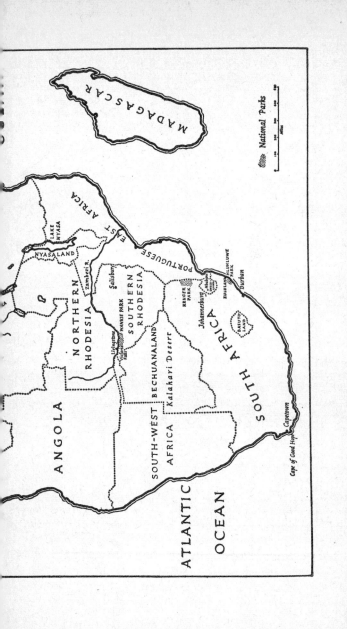

MADAGASCAR

National Parks

0   100   200   300   400   500   600
Miles

ANGOLA

NORTHERN
RHODESIA

Zambezi R.

LAKE
NYASA

NYASALAND

EAST AFRICA

Salisbury

SOUTHERN
RHODESIA

WANKIE PARK

Livingstone

Victoria
Falls

PORTUGUESE

SOUTH-WEST
AFRICA

BECHUANALAND

Kalahari Desert

KRUGER
PARK

Johannesburg

BASUTO-
LAND

SOUTH AFRICA

Cape of Good Hope

Capetown

ATLANTIC

OCEAN

HLUHLUWE
PARK

Durban

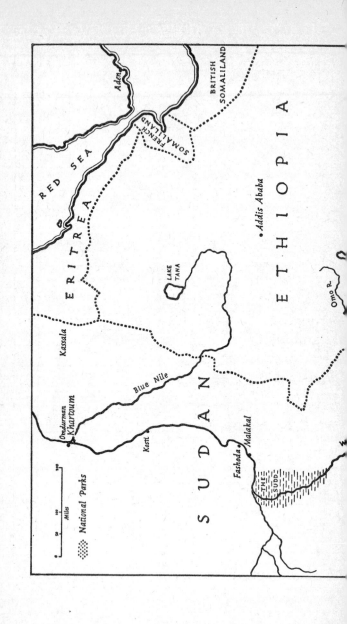

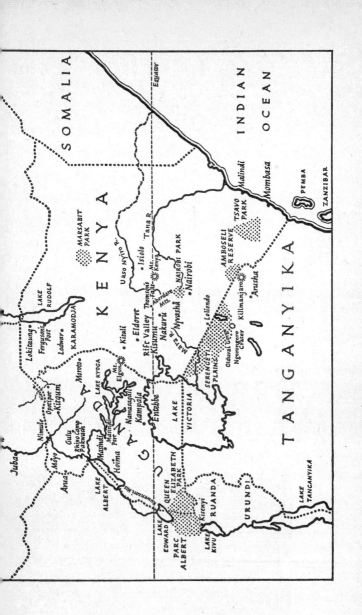